# DRAVIDIAN GODS IN MODERN HINDUISM

# DRAVIDIAN GODS IN MODERN HINDUISM

A STUDY OF THE LOCAL AND VILLAGE DEITIES OF SOUTHERN INDIA

WILBER THEODORE ELMORE, PH.D.

GYAN

*Published by*

Gyan Publishing House
5, Ansari Road
Daryaganj, New Delhi-110002
Phone: 011-47034999, 9811692060
E-mail: books@gyanbooks.com

*Distribution Network*
gyanbooks.com
India, USA, Canada, UK, Australia, France



ISBN: 978-81212-9350-1 (PB)
First Published, 1915

2nd Impression 2023

*Printed at:* Gyan Press, Delhi.



**DRAVIDIAN GODS IN MODERN HINDUISM**

AUTHOR: WILBER THEODORE ELMORE

PLATE I

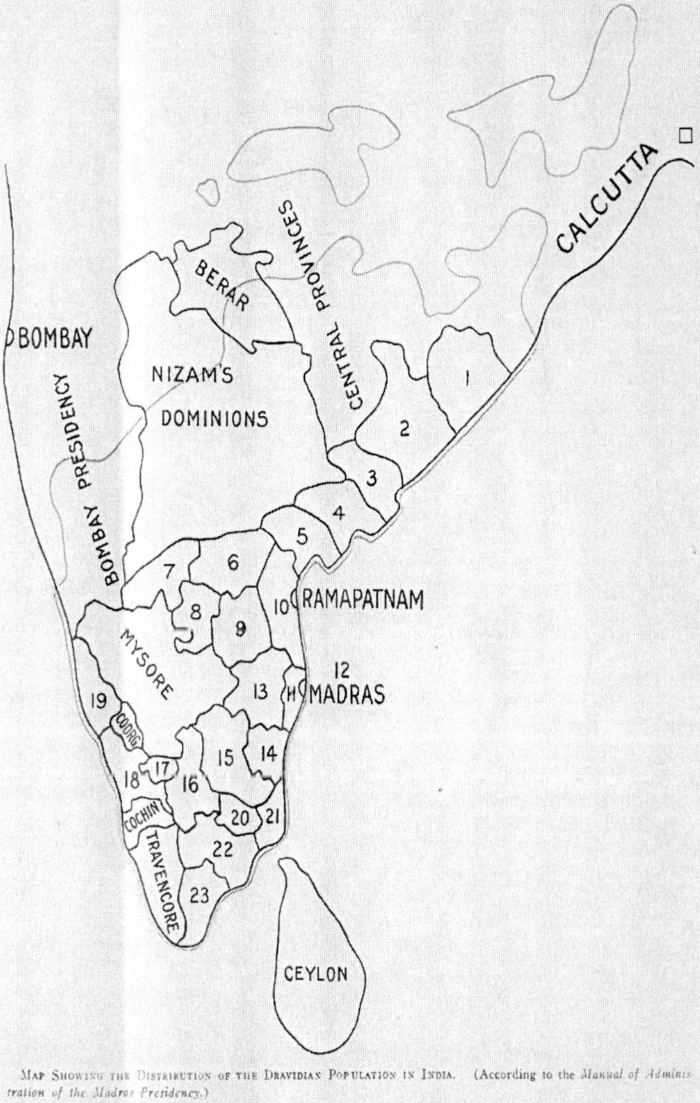


MAP SHOWING THE DISTRIBUTION OF THE DRAVIDIAN POPULATION IN INDIA. (According to the *Manual of Administration of the Madras Presidency.*)

Scale, 200 miles = 1 inch.

The portion of India in which the Dravidian population is in excess of the Aryan is surrounded by a red line.

Districts of the Madras Presidency: 1. Ganjam, 2. Vizagapatam, 3. Godavari, 4. Kistna, 5. Guntur, 6. Kurnool, 7. Bellary, 8. Anantapur, 9. Cuddapah, 10. Nellore, 11. Chingleput, 12. Madras, 13. North Arcot, 14. South Arcot, 15. Salem, 16. Coimbatore, 17. Nilgiris, 18. Malabar, 19. South Canara, 20. Trichinopoly, 21. Tanjore, 22. Madura, 23. Tinnevelly.

# DRAVIDIAN GODS IN MODERN HINDUISM

## A STUDY OF THE LOCAL AND VILLAGE DEITIES OF SOUTHERN INDIA

BY

WILBER THEODORE ELMORE, PH.D.

Reprinted from the UNIVERSITY STUDIES OF THE UNIVERSITY OF NEBRASKA,
Vol. XV, No. 1, 1915

PUBLISHED BY THE AUTHOR
HAMILTON, N. Y.
1915

# PREFATORY NOTE

The following thesis is a study of the gods of Dravidian origin which are found in Modern Hinduism. The author has resided in India almost continuously since 1900, associating somewhat closely with the people, and attempting to learn as much as possible about their various customs. During 1909–10, while pursuing studies in the department of political science and sociology of the University of Nebraska, the investigations reported in this thesis were undertaken at the suggestion of Dr. Hutton Webster, of that department. The greater part of the work has been done since the author's return to India in 1911.

The author wishes to express his gratitude to the many friends whose coöperation has made this work possible. Especial acknowledgments are due to Dr. Hutton Webster for reading the manuscript and making invaluable suggestions; to Mocherla Robert, through whose untiring efforts a considerable portion of the material has been secured; and to J. A. Curtis, who has read the manuscript and who, from his accurate knowledge of the Indian people, has rendered great assistance in verifying and interpreting the customs described.

W. T. E.

RAMAPATNAM, INDIA.
November, 1913.

# CONTENTS

# INTRODUCTION

There is no lack of authoritative works on Hinduism as a system of religion. No other system, with the exception of Christianity, is so interesting, so fully known, or has attracted so many to its study. With such abundant interest, it seems somewhat strange that a great branch of nominal Hinduism has been very largely neglected in these works. This branch is the worship of local and village deities. It is estimated,[1] and probably conservatively, that eighty per cent of the people of South India address their worship almost exclusively to such minor deities, and yet these deities receive little attention in studies of Hinduism. Often they are dismissed with a page or two, while the remainder of the treatment is given to the Brahmanic deities.[2]

The reasons for this apparent neglect are not difficult to discover. There is no systematized teaching connected with village cults or worship. No interesting systems of philosophy lie behind them. The Dravidians are not a literary people, and their religion has no literature. There are no Vedas or other writings telling of their gods. Their history is contained in the somewhat confused legends recited by wandering singers who attend the festivals and assist in the worship.

These legends and stories are always recited from memory; and as usually the singers cannot read, written stories would be of no value to them. Many of the legends, however, are written on books made from the leaves of the palmyra palm,[3] but such books are jealously guarded, and any suggestion as to translating or printing them meets with strong objections.

This worship is found largely among uneducated people, and

[1] *Madras Government Museum, Bulletin*, V, no. 3, p. 174.

[2] Sir Monier Monier-Williams, *Brahmanism and Hinduism*, London, 1891, gives the best account, Chs. VII, VIII, IX. Edward Washburn Hopkins, *The Religions of India*, London, 1895, Ch. XVIII, gives a short account of the Religious Traits of the Wild Tribes of India, under which heading he classifies this worship.

[3] Brab tree or Fan Palm tree, *Borassus flabelliformis*.

not only are they unable to give any connected account of their gods or the principles of their worship, but as soon as they see any systematic attempt being made to learn of these things they are filled with superstitious fears, and it is almost impossible to get them to tell what they do know.[4]

Again, the educated people of the land know little about these local gods, and affect to know less. Any questions are met with the reply that their worship belongs to outcastes and the lower orders of society, and that they know nothing about it. The Brahmans have a considerable interest in these gods, as will be seen later, and no doubt know far more than they are willing to admit. They are ashamed of their connection with this worship and of their fears of the gods. Then, too, since this worship is almost exclusively that of propitiation to avert some evil which a local god may be perpetrating or intending, the Brahmans do not wish to run the risk of incurring the displeasure of a god by careless remarks about it, or even of attracting its attention by allusions to it. They therefore pretend complete ignorance.

For these reasons the difficulties of learning about the subject are considerable. The material, while almost limitless, is very fugitive. There is scarcely any other way to gain necessary information than by protracted residence in India, by securing one point at a time, by coming into as close contact with the people as possible, by observing their worship, by learning as much as possible about each local deity met with, and obtaining one story here and another there. The reasons for the customs are quite commonly unknown to the people themselves, and it requires persistent effort to discover what traditions, former practices, and subconscious ideas are responsible for a great deal that takes place.

Another reason for lack of investigation in regard to these Dravidian gods is that the subject has not been considered an attractive one. There is no historic leader or founder around whose personality any interesting facts or legends may cluster. It is not a worship that any one is proud of, or that any one of

[4] In my investigations I have found that the people often thought that I was collecting facts for the Government,—an idea which filled them with needless fright.

ordinary enlightenment attempts to defend. In fact, it would not be classed by most people as coming within the range of the study of Comparative Religion, but would be assigned to Anthropology, or discussed in connection with primitive customs. Educated Indians have not cared to undertake this study, and the foreigners who write on Hinduism usually confine themselves to what they can learn from the sacred books of the Hindus, or from the educated classes.

A further obstacle lies in the fact that even if a foreigner is inclined to do field work and make personal investigations, many of the rites and ceremonies are performed at such times and in such places that it is almost impossible to conduct satisfactory research, and some of the orgies are of such a nature that, even if one had the opportunity, it would take strong nerves and some bravery to observe what is going on.[5]

While the following pages deal with Dravidian worship as found in all of southern India, the collection of new material has been confined almost exclusively to the Telugu people, and among them the larger part of the work has been done in the Nellore District. The sources of information have been largely oral. The writer has visited as many temples and places of worship as possible, and has had opportunity to see many of the ceremonies. It has usually been possible to secure some friendly person to explain what was seen. There is no reason to doubt the reliability of these explanations. It is a common experience to have those interested in the ceremonies refuse to tell about them, but I have not yet discovered any definite attempt to deceive or to fabricate an explanation. Often they evade all questions, saying that they do not know, or that this is the way their fathers did, but no deliberate deception is attempted.

Much information has been secured by conversation with people,

[5] William Crooke, *Things Indian*, New York, 1906, p. 412, says, "The subject of the Sakti sacrifices is repulsive, and few Englishmen care to explore those shrines of Kali or Devi, which reek with the blood of victims. . . . Those who are curious in such matters will refer to Ward's account of the Bengal sacrifices. . . . Dr. Oldfield gives a distressing account." This is a fair example of the feeling of most writers on Hinduism.

at other than festival times, about the various features of the worship. Priests and those directly connected with the deities, are usually not very communicative, and what they tell is fragmentary. Many facts have been verified in this way, but very little consecutive description has been secured. Among those who have left this worship, many old men can give a great deal of information. It is a tribute to the advancing intelligence and enlightenment in India that those young men whose fathers no longer worship the Dravidian deities, know almost nothing about the ceremonies.

Another method employed in collecting material was to send out a questionnaire in both Telugu and English to a large number of people who have opportunity to know about the subject under investigation. In these replies, especially those from Indian people, a great deal of useful information has been secured. Still another method, which has proved most fruitful, was to employ and train a young man for the special work of making investigations and collecting information. He soon became an expert, and was able to secure a great deal which would have been entirely beyond the reach of the personal investigations of the writer.

The written sources of information about Dravidian gods and worship are limited. The most important are the government gazetteers, district manuals, and bulletins of the Madras Government Museum. The Government of India is doing a valuable work in collecting and publishing information about the varied peoples of India and their many peculiar customs. This information is collected by district officers or by men especially selected for such purposes.

There is only one of these various reports which deals directly with the subject of this thesis. This is the Madras Government Bulletin, V, 3, by Henry Whitehead, Bishop of Madras. He has made an extensive study of village deities, and has collected a large amount of information. The other reports have various accounts of worship, demon possession, and similar matters, scattered through many pages of description of the people.

The general works which are named in the bibliography contain a great deal of material which is necessary to an understanding of the subject, especially in its relations to other forms of Hinduism. Some of these works include chapters bearing directly on the subject of these minor deities and demons. The sacred books of the Hindus hereinafter cited contain legends which have become attached to the Dravidian gods, and which often throw much light on the mutual relations of these two forms of Hinduism.

Since the material for this thesis has been gathered from so many sources, it has not been difficult to determine its reliability. In oral information, the reports have naturally very much overlapped one another, and thus made it possible to verify doubtful points. The government reports have been especially useful for verifying the information secured orally, as also have been some portions of the general works.

The importance of some knowledge of this subject to those who wish to understand modern Hinduism, and especially to those whose work brings them into direct touch with the people of India, it is scarcely necessary to emphasize. Religion to the Indian is not an external or indifferent matter. It enters into every detail of his life. It is evident, therefore, that for any sympathetic understanding of the people a knowledge of their religion is necessary. It is estimated that more than two hundred million of the people of India are of Dravidian ancestry, and while they are classified as Hindus and have adopted Hindu forms and names, their daily religion is that of their Dravidian ancestors.

# DRAVIDIAN GODS IN MODERN HINDUISM

## CHAPTER I

### The Conquest of the Dravidians

The term Dravidian is commonly used to refer to all of the non-Aryan population in the peninsula of India. The Dravidians are considered to be the aboriginal inhabitants of the land. They predominate in the southern and eastern parts of India,[1] but form a considerable part of the population in the northwestern part where the Aryans predominate.[2]

The history of the Dravidians is lost in antiquity. Long before the Aryans came to India they were the domiciled inhabitants. They have preserved no literature and left no monuments which throw light upon their origin.

There are two main theories with regard to the origin of the Dravidians in India.[3] The one most commonly accepted is that they came through the northwest passages in the Himalaya Mountains at some time far earlier than the Aryan invasion. The physiognomy of the Dravidians is very similar to that of the Caucasians, and has but little resemblance to the Mongolians. Moreover, their distribution in India would indicate that they once covered the entire land and were driven to the south and east by the later invasion of the Aryans.

The other theory is that the Dravidians have had a southern origin. The hypothetical sunken continent in the Indian Ocean, called Lemuria, is thought to have been their original home.[4] Ceylon is certainly Dravidian, and the distribution of Dravidians in India lends itself quite as well to the support of a southern origin as of a northern. The negritic type which is so often ob-

1 See map.

2 For a discussion of the distribution of Dravidian languages see R. Caldwell, *A Comparative Grammar of the Dravidian or South Indian Family of Languages*, London, 1875, Introduction.

3 For a full discussion of the origin of the Dravidians in India see *The Manual of Administration of the Madras Presidency*, 1885, I, pp. 29 sq.

4 See W. Crooke, *The Northwest Provinces of India*, London, 1897, pp. 198 sq.

served, especially in the Yanadis,[5] has been attributed to this southern origin, but it is probable that for centuries coasting traders have gone back and forth between India and Africa. The monsoon winds blowing steadily for many weeks every year from the southwest to India, may also have brought shipwrecked Africans or those who put out too far to sea and were unable to get back to land.

It is not the intention of this thesis to throw new light on the question of the origin of the Dravidians. It is sufficient to point out that when the Aryan invaders came to India they found another race in possession of the land—a race which they gradually subjugated, and to some extent assimilated.

In South India the Aryans are now represented almost exclusively by the Brahmans. It is usually understood that of the four castes of Hinduism, the Sudras only are Dravidian, but it is probable that very few people in South India who claim descent from the Vaisyas and Kshatriyas are of Aryan origin.[6] The Komaties, or merchants, claim to be Vaisyas, but there appears to be an intimate connection between them and the Madigas, or leather workers, who are of undoubted Dravidian origin.[7] When a marriage takes place among the Komaties it is necessary to bring the fire from the house of a Madiga for the new household. Many devices are used to cover up this connection. A Komatie will come on some pretext to the house of a Madiga, and after completing his business will ask for a light for his cheroot. Komaties, however, do not deny the connection.

The hymns of the Rigveda[8] give us much light on the great struggle of the Aryans in conquering the Dravidians. The Aryans

[5] *Madras Government Museum, Bulletin,* IV, no. 2, pp. 87 sq. gives a full discussion of the probable origin of the Yanadis.

[6] Thurston, *Castes and Tribes of Southern India,* IV, pp. 79 sq., for "Kshatriya"; VII, pp. 271, sq., for "Vaisya."

[7] *Ibid.,* III, pp. 325 sq.

[8] See especially the following hymns of the *Rigveda*: T. H. Griffith, *The Ramayan of Valmiki,* Benares. 1895, Book I, Cantos 22, 117, 132, 175. Book II, Canto 20. Book III, Canto 53. Book IV, Cantos 6, 16, 28, 30, 32. Book V, Canto 7. Book VI, Cantos 23, 25, 31. Book VII, Canto 99. Book VIII, Canto 14. Book IX, Canto 41. Book X, Cantos 22, 29.

PLATE II

YANADIS

The Negritic type is unequivocal in this group.

TYPES OF DRAVIDIAN FACES

These people are Sudras. Negritic features are absent in this type.

were not lacking in epithets with which to describe these people. They called them "enemies," "slaves," "abject tribes," "void of sense," "inhuman," "keeping alien rites," "malignant," "wicked," "riteless," "prayerless," "bestowing no gifts" (to the gods), "pouring no oblation of milk," "non-worshipers," "priestless," "not keeping sacred fires," "worshipers of mad gods," and they even accused them of eating human flesh.

It is probable that this is an exaggerated description, for the conquerors also speak of their enemies as being wealthy in herds, having impregnable castles, forts of iron, and cities. They were found to be most powerful foes, and probably were stubborn in their resistance, as the Aryans called them "bull-jawed." In the course of time, however, the conquest was complete. The Aryans became the rulers, and the Dravidians took a subordinate position in the newly organized caste system.

The conquerors soon found that if they were to hold the Dravidians in subjection some consideration for their religion was necessary. Although the Dravidians were worshipers of "mad gods," they were most tenacious of their religious rites. The Aryans did not attempt to compel them to give up their gods, but adopted the policy of bringing the people with their religion into the fold of Hinduism. This process has been going on until the present time.[9] To what extent the effort has succeeded is evident on every hand.[10]

[9] *Gazetteer of Vizagapatam District,* I. p. 75. The Khonds, a hill tribe, are an illustration. They are still worshipping simultaneously their aboriginal god, Poleramma from the Telugu country, and an orthodox Hindu god.

[10] *Census of 1911,* Vol. XII, Pt. I. Ch. 4, (paras. 4, 6, 22, 26). "It is well to remember that the strict connotation of the word Hinduism is racial and social rather than theological. At the same time we may admit that Hinduism is in a sense acquisitive. If it strains out the individual gnat, it can swallow with cheerfulness the tribal camel. Some slight profession of faith, and modern efficiency in the nice conduct of ceremony, are sufficient to secure for an aspiring animistic tribe, gods included, admission within the pale.

"The most debatable Hindu may well worship, and often does worship, the great Hindu deities. Such worship is not a necessary impediment to a simultaneous worship of many minor godlings. The two acts of faith at times co-exist even in Brahmans.

"Whatever may be their present-day union or interminglement, it is difficult to imagine any original connection of the Aryan Brahmans and their

The original Vedic religion finds but little in common with modern Hinduism. The great mass of Dravidian deities, rites, and superstitions have become a part of so-called Hinduism, and while somewhat changed by Brahmanic Hinduism, the latter has been equally changed by the Dravidian religion.[11]

subtle philosophies, with the gross demonolatry of the Dravidian peoples who surrounded them. Holding certain philosophical opinions, which they neither expected nor particularly desired their Dravidian neighbors to share, it is unlikely that the early Aryan theorists made any serious efforts to obtain adherents to their way of thinking. But satisfied with the admission of their undoubted intellectual superiority, they built gradually many a connecting bridge between their own somewhat unpractical speculations, and the extremely materialistic demonologies of the Dravidians."

E. A. Gait, Census Commissioner for India, in his "Notes on Census Returns of Hindus," dated Simla, 12th July, 1910 (See *Indian Social Reformer*, Bombay, Nov. 20, 1912), discusses at length the question as to who are to be enumerated as Hindus. "The complaint has often been made that the Census returns of Hindus are misleading, as they include millions of people who are not really Hindus at all, who are denied the ministrations of the Brahmans, and are forbidden to enter Hindu temples, and who in many cases are regarded as so unclean that their touch, or even their proximity, causes pollution. There is of course much truth in the criticism, but the fact that Hinduism has no definite creed makes it difficult to lay down any definite test as to who is, and who is not a Hindu. A man may believe in the whole Hindu pantheon, or only in particular gods, or, for that matter, in no gods at all; he may sacrifice or abstain from sacrifices; he may eat flesh and fish or abstain from so doing; but he is still regarded as a Hindu if he belongs to a recognized Hindu caste, does not deny the supremacy of the Brahmans, and abstains from open disregard of the restrictions observed by his caste fellows." Mr. Gait proposes the following as some of the tests which might be applied to discover whether any certain class may be regarded as Hindus or not. "(1) Do the members of the caste or tribe worship the great Hindu gods? (2) Are they allowed to enter Hindu temples or make offerings at the shrine? (3) Will good Brahmans act as their priests? (4) Will degraded Brahmans do so? In that case, are they recognized as Brahmans by persons outside the caste, or are they Brahmans only in name? (5) Will clean castes take water from them? (6) Do they cause pollution, (*a*) by touch, (*b*) by proximity?" These tests would cut off from Hinduism all the outcastes, who are a very considerable number in the census, and who commonly claim to be genuine Hindus.

[11] *Gazetteer of South Arcot,* I, p. 94: "The attitude of the Hindus of the district toward the numerous deities worshiped therein is an odd medley

Siva worship is a marked illustration of the adoption of aboriginal gods.[12] Siva is a god of the Puranas, and in connection with his worship there is much that is opposed to Brahmanism. He appears to be a deified chief.[13] His wife, Parvati, is more strikingly aboriginal than Siva himself. She appears in many different forms. As Kali[14] she is a bloodthirsty goddess, wearing a necklace of skulls, and dancing on the bodies of her fallen enemies. Another name commonly given her is Durga.[15] The goddesses of the Dravidians are commonly said to be incarnations of Kali or Durga, and so the wives of Siva.

Ganesa, the elephant headed god, and Hanuman, the monkey god, are said to be the sons of Siva,[16] and in this way are connected

of orthodox Brahmanic ideas, and the most primitive superstitions." "A Native," *Pen and Ink Sketches of Native Life in South India*, Madras, 1880, shows the attitude of mind assumed by many of the Indians of Aryan descent toward the Dravidian people. He says, "The pariah and chuckler people and a whole lot of other half-wild tribes are supposed to be the aborigines of the country." He then tells something of their demon-worship and their subjection to the higher castes.

[12] On Siva as an aboriginal deity see Wilkins, *Hindu Mythology*, Calcutta, 1882, p. 280; *The Manual of Administration of the Madras Presidency*, I, p. 84; *Journal of the Ethnological Society*, I, p. 96.

[13] Sir Alfred C. Lyall, *Asiatic Studies*, London, 1907, First Series, p. 49. Sir Monier Monier-Williams, *Brahmanism and Hinduism*, London, 1891, p. 84.

[14] Kali is the tutelary goddess of Kalighat, from which place the city of Calcutta takes its name. Large numbers of goats and sometimes buffalos are beheaded here daily. The temple is owned by Brahmans who have become immensely wealthy through the large number of offerings made by pilgrims. For a description of the worship at Kalighat see Shib Chundar Bose, *The Hindus as They Are*, Calcutta, 1883, pp. 133 sq.

[15] Gustav Oppert, *The Original Inhabitants of India*, Westminster, 1893, p. 495. Kali as Durga sometimes receives the buffalo sacrifice in South India. She has every mark of an aboriginal deity.

[16] Hanuman is also claimed by the Vaishnavas. For the legend of his double parentage see Moor, *The Hindu Pantheon*, Madras, 1864, pp. 250 sq. *The Manual of Administration of the Madras Presidency*, I, p. 72, says that monkeys were always worshiped in India, and when Siva worship came, the old monkey god, Hanuman, was called an incarnation of Siva. *The Travencore State Manual*, II, p. 51, classifies these gods as tutelary deities.

with the Hindu pantheon. It is possible that they were totems or tribal animal gods of some branch of the aborigines, and have been adopted into Hinduism.

It appears that this adoption of aboriginal gods under the guise of Siva worship has never fully satisfied either Brahmans or Dravidians. There is evidence in the Nellore District that Siva worship was once far stronger than at present. On every hand fallen temples may be found, and these are almost invariably Siva temples. They are usually found in the fields at some little distance from the villages, and appear to have been deserted for a long time, perhaps for centuries. There are no local traditions of any value concerning these temples. The architecture is not to be compared with that of the temples in the towns, yet they are usually built with massive stones. They are far better buildings than the shrines of the Dravidian deities, but the style of architecture is somewhat the same.

It is probable that these temples were built by local kings at public expense, under the direction of Brahmans at court. They were built in the fields to satisfy the customs of the people, and the style was Dravidian rather than Aryan. With the coming of political changes support by the government disappeared, except in cases where lands had been given to the temples, and the small Siva temples seem not to have been thus endowed. As now the burden of keeping up the worship fell upon the people themselves, they found the Siva worship too much Brahmanized to suit their tastes, and they soon went back to their unchanged Dravidian gods.

Although Siva has been deserted, the village demonesses are usually said to be his wives. His sons, Hanuman and Ganesa, also seem to be nearer to the hearts of the people. The image of Hanuman is commonly worn around the necks of the children, being drawn on a small piece of metal, while a large stone image of Ganesa is often found beside the shrine of the Dravidian village goddess, and at times is even placed in the temple beside the goddess.

It is evident, therefore, that although much of the aboriginal religion and many of the gods have been adopted into Hinduism, working great changes in Hinduism itself, there has been but very little assimilation in the thoughts and customs of the people. In many ways an artificial connection has been found between the original Dravidian worship and Hinduism, and the people are classified as Hindus, but the connection is to a great extent in name only. The same strange rites, the same basal beliefs and ideas, which these Dravidians possessed tens of centuries ago, seem no less powerful to-day. The Dravidians have been conquered politically and socially, but religiously the contact of Aryans and Dravidians has resulted in not more than a drawn battle.[17]

[17] *Gazetteer of Madura District*, I. 84, states that in many places in this district the influence of the Brahmans is comparatively weak, and that weddings are performed without the help of these intermediaries. The fact is very unusual, and shows that Brahmans have not secured complete control. In the Madura District they are only 18 in every 1000 of the population. *The Manual of Administration of the Madras Presidency*, I, p. 71, gives a story to the effect that to subdue Vishnu, Siva placed himself at the head of the demoniacal aborigines. This story indicates some early struggle before Siva became a Hindu god. The Dravidian goddess, Ellamma, is sometimes represented with the torn-off head of a Brahman in her hand, which indicates that the political conquest was not an easy one. See Oppert, *Original Inhabitants of India*, p. 464.

## CHAPTER II

### General Features of Dravidian Worship

Hinduism as commonly known, and as described in the various treatises on the subject, is the religion which originated in Vedic times. It is controlled entirely by the Brahmans. The prominent temples which are so evident in every town and village, are temples for Vishnu or Siva or some of their incarnations or avatars.

Rama, the hero of the Ramayana, an avatar of Vishnu, is met in every village, and has become to some extent a tutelary god of South India.[1] His shrine is often small and poorly built, probably because he is considered much in the same light as the Dravidian gods.

In all Vishnu and Siva temples Brahman priests officiate. The worship has something more of dignity and mystery than that of the Dravidian gods, but it cannot be said to be a popular worship. This worship is supported largely through endowments of lands made to the temples in former days by kings who wished to be friendly with the Brahmans, or to attain merit for themselves. These lands are now usually under the control of the government, and the income is paid for the expenses of the temples. Pilgrims and people hoping to attain merit also make gifts for the support of the temples.

The mass of the people, meanwhile, are giving their attention almost exclusively to another group of gods. Near every village may be seen small rude temples or shrines. Usually an unhewn stone or a crudely graven image is the only occupant, and to these

[1] *The Manual of Administration of the Madras Presidency*, I, 71, gives an interesting fact that the Shanans ('toddy-drawers') of South India still celebrate with joy the successes of Ravana and the defeat of Rama. At one time I was watching the removal of a fallen Ramaswami shrine in a hamlet where his worship had ceased, and beneath the image were found shells and little pots used in Dravidian devil worship. Also one Chinese cash was found! The history of this is a mystery. It is evident that when Rama's shrine was erected, the people felt safer to have the symbols of their demons included also.

images the people pay their devotions. There is also another class of images which may very seldom be seen. These are temporary images which are made for worship on a single occasion, and then are deserted or thrown away.

Practically all of the people except the Brahmans join actively in the worship of these minor gods, and the Brahmans are by no means indifferent. The most of the sacrifices are of slaughtered animals, hence usually a Brahman will not act as priest. An occasional exception, however, is found. The Brahmans quite commonly direct some parts of the worship, and often are present, usually standing at a distance.[2] They admit that these deities are powerful demons, and so are not to be neglected. One Brahman of education explained his position in the matter to an English official as follows: "I attempt to win the favor of the collector because he may promote me, but I pay blackmail to the Kollans too. Of what good is the collector's friendship if the Kollans steal my bullocks?"[3] In his illustration the collector represented the Brahmanic deities and the Kollans the minor gods and demons.

The characteristics which distinguish these Dravidian deities from the Brahmanic gods are in general as follows.[4] In the first place the Brahmanic gods usually have some kind of a divine history. They have some legendary birth in the abode of the gods, and appear on the earth in various avatars. The Dravidian gods, however, are usually local in their origin. Their history commonly begins on earth, often as the ghost of some person who has died. In the thought of the people also, the Dravidian gods are local. Each village has its own deity, a fact which has given rise to the common term of "Village Deities" for these Dravidian

[2] At a great festival for Kulagollamma in Kavili, Nellore District, Sept. 5, 1913, I saw large numbers of Brahmans standing on an elevation watching the beheading of buffaloes and the drawing of the carts. I talked with some of them, asking them how it was that they were consenting to the bloody offerings. They replied that in a time of danger it was right to take life. The present danger was that Kulagollamma would send cholera if not propitiated.

[3] *Gazetteer of Tanjore*, I, p. 67.

[4] *Madras Government Museum, Bulletin*, V, no. 3, p. 109. J. N. Farquahar, *A Primer of Hinduism*, London, 1911, pp. 153 sq.

gods. Even when one god is found in many places, the people never think of it as a general god with world relations, but only as their local deity.

Again, these gods are almost always propitiated with bloody or animal sacrifices, but this is not the case with true Hindu gods. Because of these bloody sacrifices, and also for historical reasons, the *pujari*, or priest, is very rarely a Brahman. The Dravidian deities, moreover, are commonly of the female sex, in contrast to the masculine nature of the Hindu gods.

In India there are exceptions to all rules, and so every one of the above tests will be found to fail at times. But the whole character of these Dravidian deities and their worship is so marked, that there is no danger of confusing the two.[5] The people themselves commonly distinguish between the gods of Dravidian and of Hindu origin, although they cannot tell what is the basis of their classification. It is a striking phenomenon that after centuries of close contact and definite efforts to amalgamate the two cults, the breach seems almost as wide to-day as ever it was, as far as rites and basic beliefs are concerned.[6]

[5] *Manual of Administration of the Madras Presidency*, I, p. 70, divides the deities of India into three classes: (1) Brahmanic deities, (2) Aboriginal deities, and (3) Deities which are a combination of these two. In the case of the last-named deities it is not difficult to trace their origin either to Brahmanic or aboriginal sources, and to discover how the other element has been added.

[6] The *Gazetteer of South Arcot District*, I, p. 375, gives a strange instance of an exception to the rule that these gods are female. In the town of Kuvnakkam is a god named Aravan. There is a tradition concerning him which is found in the Tamil version of the *Mahabharata*, but not in the Sanskrit original, that Aravan was a man who offered his life as a sacrifice to assist the Pandavas when they were in despair because their enemies had offered a white elephant. He was deified, and now men dress as women at his festival, vow to marry him, and bewail him as their husband. This is without doubt Dravidian, even though the god is not female. Other exceptions will be noticed in the various descriptions of the deities.

## CHAPTER III

### The Seven Sisters

In all parts of South India the Seven Sisters are the most prominent among Dravidian deities. They have one younger brother called Potu Razu. His name seems to be the same everywhere, but the names of the Seven Sisters vary, localities quite near together often having different names for them. In the Kandukuru Taluq of the Nellore District the names commonly given are Poleramma, Ankamma, Muthyalamma, Dilli Polasi, Bangaramma, Mathamma, and Renuka. Of these Poleramma is the best known, being found in almost every village.[1]

As the worship of the Seven Sisters is typical of that of all the Dravidian deities, the rites connected with each will be described with some detail.

Poleramma. The temple or shrine of Poleramma is usually outside the village, and quite frequently on the bank of an irrigation tank, or reservoir.[2] The shrine is usually very crude, sometimes built with stones and mud. At other times it consists of

[1] For other lists see *Madras Government Museum, Bulletin*, V, no. 3, p. 116; *Manual of Administration of Madras Presidency*, I, p. 78; Oppert, *Original Inhabitants of India*, p. 488. Oppert includes two wives of Iyenar, thus making nine in his group. Pidari in his list appears to be Poleramma.

[2] Bishop Whitehead classifies Poleramma as a "boundary goddess." See *Madras Government Museum, Bulletin*, V, no. 3. p. 111. *Polimeru* is a Telugu word meaning 'boundary,' or more accurately the field between two villages. It is probable that the similarity of names, and the fact that Poleramma's temple is outside the village, have given the impression that she is a boundary goddess. J. A. Curtis of Donokonda writes, "I am unable to confirm my impression that Poleramma is a boundary goddess. Baita Ankamma also is related to the boundaries. Of course *polimeru* means not the edge of the settlement, but the field boundary between two separate villages. In this sense the Poleramma temple is not on the boundary." Regarding boundary goddesses the *Gazetteer of South Arcot District*, I, p. 92, says, "In many places stone slabs may be seen set up on the outskirts of the village on what are said to be the old boundaries." Some of these have become idols. On others cocoanuts are broken annually.

stones two or three feet long, set upright in the ground on three sides of a small square, the fourth side being left open. On the top is placed a flat stone. Within the shrine will be found one small plain stone, of no particular form, set upright in the ground. This is the image of Poleramma. Very rarely Poleramma will have a temple built after the pattern of those Siva temples which are found in the fields.

Poleramma is the goddess of smallpox in the Telugu country, as Mariammam is in the Tamil country. She is also considered to be responsible to some extent for all other troubles in the village, such as cattle disease, drought, and sickness among the people. The name Poleramma, however, is the common expression among the people for smallpox.[3]

When smallpox breaks out in a village, the people say that Poleramma has come to them. She is supposed to be angry, and expresses her anger by the disease. Before a general *jatara*, or the offering of bloody sacrifices to appease the goddess, takes place, the afflicted person performs certain propitiatory ceremonies.

The first thing done is to place some cactus leaves on the wall near the gate. Sometimes the cactus is placed over the door.[4] The intention in this is that Poleramma, seeing the cactus, will think the place uninhabited and pass on, since cactus would not be allowed to grow on the wall of an inhabited house. Then a sheep or small buffalo is tied to the leg of the cot on which the sick man is lying. If the people are very poor, a chicken will be substituted. This animal is a votive offering, and it is hoped that with this promise Poleramma will be satisfied and leave the house.

Whether the smallpox disappears or not, within a few days the devoted animal is taken outside the village boundaries and sacrificed. Two pots of food are prepared. Some of the food is placed on the decapitated head of the buffalo, or other animal sac-

[3] *Ammavaru*, a respectful title for a woman, is a name also given to smallpox. In some places *Peddamma* meaning a great woman, is used for smallpox, and *Chinnamma* meaning a lesser woman, is used for chickenpox. In every case the underlying meaning is the same, that of a female deity bringing the disease. See *Brown's English-Telugu Dictionary*, Madras, 1903, p. 1187. Here *ammavaru* is translated "our lady."

[4] This is done also for cholera, and at times for other diseases.

PLATE III

POLERAMA

This is a fair example of a Dravidian goddess when the image is carved and dressed. More commonly the image is an uncarved stone.

rificed, and the head with the food on it is left outside the boundaries, with the hope that Poleramma also will be pleased to remain outside. The remainder of the food is taken home by the one offering it, and is eaten there. When smallpox has appeared in a village, many of the people besides the afflicted family perform these ceremonies as a precautionary measure.

If the smallpox appears to be spreading, a general *jatara*[5] is arranged for. First the announcement of the coming *jatara* is made, and offerings solicited. This is done as follows. After bathing the image of Poleramma, a procession is formed, led by the Madiga *asadi* or story teller, a village servant called a *yetti*, and a washerman. Taking new pots these three go about the village from house to house announcing the coming *jatara*. At each house they receive a small amount of food and buttermilk, which later they divide among themselves. They then go to the centre of the village, and taking a new pot they place in it one-fourth of an *anna*,[6] some turmeric, charcoal, and rice. The *asadi* now tells the story of Poleramma, describing her powers and the dangers which may come from neglecting her. The people become much wrought up, and make vows to her to be fulfilled at the time of the *jatara*. The pot is then tied to a tree and left until the time of worship.

The *jatara* itself, or festival, usually occupies four days.[7] On the first day the pot is taken from the tree and carried in procession through the village, accompanied by the beating of drums.

[5] *Jatara* is a Dravidian word meaning originally a tumult or noisy disturbance. *Tirunalla* is also a Dravidian word meaning literally "good days." It is used also for the festivals of the gods. I find that there is much confusion in the minds of the people as to the use of these words. One will say that the festival is a *jatara*, and another that the same festival is a *tirunalla*. The most common distinction is that a *tirunalla* is the general merry-making part, and the *jatara* is the time of bloody propitiation. *Tirunalla* is often used of the worship of the Hindu gods, but *jatara* never is.

[6] An *anna* is equal to one penny or two cents.

[7] For a full description of the worship of Peddamma, which is very similar, see Bishop Whitehead's account in *Madras Government Museum, Bulletin*, V, no. 3, pp. 129 ff.; also *Kurnool District Manual*, 1880, Sec. II, pp. 150–156.

As it is carried past each house the inmates come out and bow in worship before it. All the people then bring pots of food, and going to the house of the head man of the shepherd caste, they spread leaf-plates and make an offering of food. The *asadi* summons all the elders to witness, calling each one by name, and publicly announces the various vows made to Poleramma. A sheep is then sacrificed to seal the promises made in the vows. Once again the procession forms and the pot is carried around the village, food being collected at each house. The *asadi* chants the stories of the gods as they go, telling of their various wars and exploits, in order to arouse the people to take a proper part in the worship. After collecting the food the procession goes outside the village to the temple of Poleramma. The temple is purified with various ceremonies, Poleramma is bathed, and the pot of food and some offerings are placed before her.

The procession now forms anew and goes to the water, a well or irrigation tank, where the royal staff and the snake's hood[8] have been kept in water over night. These are taken from the water, and carried to the temple, after a sheep has been offered. After placing the royal staff and snake's hood beside Poleramma in the temple another sheep is offered, and this usually completes the ceremonies of the first day.

On the second day there are still more processions about the village, and food is offered in front of the house of another shepherd. A sheep is sacrificed, and story telling continues as on the first day. The third day they start the procession earlier, and more food is collected. Those who collect the food eat it themselves, after offering it to the goddess, so this part of the ceremonies is not neglected. In the afternoon all the people leave their houses, and going to some suitable spot outside the village near the temple of Poleramma, they cook food, and eat it after offering it to Poleramma.

The merry-making part of the festival now takes place. The villagers bring their carts and oxen, the carts being gaily decorated for the occasion, and form a procession to go around the temple. Some people, especially children, ride in the carts and think this

[8] For meaning of these emblems see page 83.

is great sport. There is a definite order for the carts, according to the wealth of the owner, and his standing in the community. At times, when the number of carts is large, there is great confusion, and the beating of drums and shouting of the people make the oxen frantic. Accidents appear to be rare, however.[9]

After the procession of carts, the people bring sheep, goats, and chickens and offer them to Poleramma, carrying away the carcasses to be eaten later. This ends the ceremonies of the third day.

The fourth day is the greatest day of the festival, and has the most repulsive features of any part of the ceremonies. A great heap of boiled *cholam,* kaffir corn, is poured out before the goddess, and then the buffalo[10] sacrifice is brought. The story tellers recount the deeds of heroes, and get the people into a high state of excitement. The drums are then beaten loudly, while men seize the buffalo by head and body, pulling on it so that the neck is strained tight. The *pujari* blesses the sword and hands it to the executioner, usually a Madiga. He worships the sword, bowing to the ground before it, then with one stroke he severs the head from the body.[11] The head is then placed before Poleramma, and one, or quite commonly, both front legs are cut off at the knee and placed crosswise in the mouth of the buffalo. Some of the fat is taken from the abdomen of the buffalo and spread over its eyes, and a wick placed in a small vessel of oil is lighted and placed on the head. This oil that is burned is supposed to be from the fat of the buffalo, but this rule does not seem to be commonly observed.

Water is then poured over the blood, and later it is well cov-

[9] At one time I witnessed a procession in which the leg of an ox was broken.

[10] The Indian buffalo, *Bos bubalus.* The buffalo offered is usually a small one, perhaps a year old.

[11] It is said that the executioner is allowed three strokes, and if more are required the offering is not acceptable. If the buffalo is small, one stroke usually suffices, but with a large animal I have seen most distressing scenes when many blows were required. There was no evidence in these cases that the offering was not acceptable. The requirement seemed to be that the animal must stand until the head falls, and I have seen it held up by poles until the neck was severed.

ered with earth from fear lest some of it should be carried to another village, as this would destroy the efficacy of the sacrifice. Later the outcastes remove the body of the buffalo, which comes to them as a part of their pay for the work of the day.

At the close of the worship of Poleramma, a sheep is offered to Potu Razu, and some of the food is poured out before him. He is then requested to guard the village, and the ceremonies come to an end.

Potu Razu is represented by a small stone placed at some distance from the shrine of Poleramma. Bishop Whitehead says of him:[12] "Potu Razu is a mysterious person in the Telugu country; sometimes he is described as the brother, sometimes as the husband of the village goddess, and sometimes as only an attendant. Once I was told that he was the devil's younger brother, and occasionally the villagers seem to think that the less said about him the better. But I have never met with him as an independent deity, and have always been told that sacrifice is never offered to him alone, but always in conjunction with one or more of the goddesses."

ANKAMMA. This goddess has much in common with Poleramma. She is usually represented by a stone image in a little temple outside the village. Sometimes the image has some resemblance to a human form, but often it is an unhewn stone. In addition to this usual position, Ankamma is often a household god.[13] When she is worshiped as a household goddess she is represented by a pot in which are some shells, little earthen mugs, and other similar articles. The shells represent the teeth of devils, and the pots represent the food which they desire.

The worship of Ankamma as a village goddess is much the same as that of Poleramma, and so need not be described in detail. It is more bloody, however, and seems to increase in fervor and cruelty during the five days which it usually continues. On the first day three buffalos and three sheep are sacrificed, the blood

[12] *Madras Government Museum, Bulletin*, V, no. 3, p. 111.

[13] Any god may become a household god, but Ankamma seems to be the one most commonly chosen.

being poured out before Ankamma. At this time the drum beaters and horn blowers make a great tumult. The excitement increases as the tumult grows louder, and the people leap and dance as if possessed by demons.

On the fourth day, in memory of Papanooka, whose story will be told later,[14] a man disguised as a woman carries a paper balloon in procession on the end of a long pole. Above the balloon is a pot and above that a drinking cup, while the royal staff and snake hood are carried behind accompanied by drumming and shouting.[15]

On the last day the cruel features of the worship take place. The village carpenter prepares a rude cart on which are set stakes sharply pointed at the upper end. The usual number of stakes is nine. On these are impaled alive a goat, a pig, a lamb, a chicken, and other small animals. Then the story-teller drinks the blood of a sheep, sometimes severing the jugular vein with his teeth, and disguised as a woman mounts to the top of the cart. Here sitting on a board prepared for him, he rides to Ankamma's temple in the midst of the suffering animals. The cart is drawn with great tumult by the Madigas and Malas, while the crowd follows with beating of drums and great excitement. After they have arrived at the temple a live sheep is impaled on a stake set for that purpose in the ground in front of the temple.[16] All of these animals of course die in their agonies.

The usual explanation of the impaling of the animals is that Ankamma enters the man who is disguised as a woman, and is

[14] See page 98.

[15] The story tellers in the worship of Ankamma are called *pambala vandlu.* They are Malas. The Madiga *asadis*—who are the story-tellers for Poleramma and the most of these gods—would not be allowed to tell the story of Ankamma.

[16] Oppert, *Original Inhabitants of India,* 479, tells of another cruel practice in the worship of Mariamman, when live chickens are thrown among the crowd from the temple. The people catch them and tear them to pieces as they fall. It is claimed that the impaling ceremony is uncommon now, and that the legs of the sheep are tied together and simply hooked over the impaling stake. There is much reason to believe, however, that the impaling still goes on, especially in out of the way places,

propitiated by this suffering and shedding of blood. After these horrible ceremonies are over, food is poured out before the goddess. The people then eat, and the festival closes with the usual procession of carts about the temple.[17]

MUTHYALAMMA. The worship of this goddess is much the same as that of Poleramma. In the *jatara* for Muthyalamma which the writer was able to observe,[18] a temporary clay image was used to represent the goddess, as her own temple and image were at some distance. This temporary image was afterwards left to be trampled under foot. The object of the worship at this time was to bring rain. Three buffalos and a large number of sheep, goats, and chickens were offered.

In a case like this, where more than one buffalo is offered, the one first slain is the real buffalo sacrifice, which is so constant a feature in the worship of these gods. The remaining buffalos, like the other animals, are usually given by individuals in payment of vows. The one main buffalo sacrifice in which the head is placed before the idol, is an essential of a *jatara*. This sacrifice is for the entire village. Other offerings are optional.

DILLI POLASI. This goddess also is both a village and a household deity. As a household goddess she is represented by a number of pots placed one on top of another, the largest at the bottom, and hung in a network of rope. These pots are very commonly seen in any village house.

The household worship is simple. Usually the mother of the wife of the household will send new clothes to her daughter and son-in-law. They put these on, tie the ends together, and sit near the household god, while the village story-teller, dressed as a Brahman, gives a forecast of the coming year, the rain, the crops, the prosperity of the farm and herds. He imitates a Brahman in reading their horoscopes, and the prophecy is usually a favorable one. The husband and wife are then remarried. The wife removes her *tali bottu*, or marriage symbol, which is worn around her neck. The story-teller, now acting as priest, fur-

[17] Ankamma is also called Ankallamma. In Tamil she is Angaramma.

[18] In Ramapatnam, May, 1907. Muthyalamma is the village goddess of Ramapatnam.

PLATE IV

THE SACRED MUGGU

These *muggus* are in preparation for a feast, and are not so much for use in the worship as for ornament. The *muggus* described in the text are of the same nature, but not often so large. Those designed for ornament are made by the women of the household, and not by a priest. The picture is of a Brahman home.

PREPARING THE SACRIFICIAL FEAST

This is the feast which is eaten in connection with the worship of Dravidian deities. It is prepared in a grove. The sheep is decorated with leaves as an offering to the goddess. It will be killed before the idol and afterwards will be eaten.

nishes a new string, and her husband again ties it around her neck as he did on the first wedding day. They then worship Dilli Polasi, eat together, and this rather pleasing ceremony is at an end.

The public worship of Dilli Polasi is more often engaged in by one family, or a group of related families, than by all the village. For this worship an earthen image is made, which is afterwards allowed to fall to pieces in sun and rain. The head of the worshiping family acts as priest. The pots and ropes are taken to the water, and after ceremonies for purification, are left there all night, a watch having been placed to see that they are not molested or defiled.

In the morning the head of the family summons all of the relatives. A sheep is sacrificed, and then they go to the water. Here they make the *muggu*[19] on the ground and sacrifice another sheep. The ropes and pots are then taken from the water and carried in procession through the village. When the house is reached another sheep is sacrificed. The executioner cuts its throat and then taking it by the rear legs, he swings it around several times. This is an offering to the evil spirits which may be hovering about in the air. It is hoped that, satisfied with the gift, they will not attempt to enter the house.

The people then enter the house and worship the earthen image of Dilli Polasi. The story-telling begins, and if the family is able to hire a story-teller of ability, it may continue for several days, much to the delight of the entire community.

BANGARAMMA. This goddess does not seem to be so important as some of her sisters. Very commonly she has no temple of her own, but her image is placed in the temple of Poleramma. At times she has a smaller temple near that of Poleramma, and receives a small share of the worship when that goddess is propitiated.

19 A *muggu* is a pattern of various designs commonly drawn before the doors of houses for ornamentation. It is made with lime or rice flour which the women sift through their fingers very deftly in making the pattern. The same name is given to a sacred pattern which is used in many parts of the worship, especially in exorcism of devils, as will be seen later. This sacred *muggu* is made by the one officiating as priest.

The worship of Bangaramma has much in common with that of Poleramma. It begins, however, very mildly. There may be some connection between the name Bangaramma, meaning "the golden one," and her mild nature. The first day the children are treated to sweetmeats, and have a general good time. After this pleasant beginning, however, the people seem to forget that she is different from the others, and the *jatara* increases in intensity until it comes to resemble that of the other goddesses.

The buffalo sacrifice takes place on the third day. After the severed head is placed before Bangaramma, water is poured over it until the head is said to jump. This indicates that the sacrifice is acceptable to Bangaramma, and the people dance like demons while the drums and horns keep up the wildest din.

A strange custom is now observed. The Madigas, who are outcastes, begin to revile the caste people, using the vilest language. They certainly are adepts at invective, and make good use of their opportunity. The caste people not only expect this berating, but demand it. If the Madigas show any reluctance to begin, the caste people will beat them with ropes and sticks to compel them to perform their duty. No doubt the Madigas get a good deal of satisfaction out of this privilege and pay off many an old score, for they are in the position of serfs to the higher castes, and often suffer a good deal of oppression.

MATHAMMA AND MATANGI. Mathamma is the especial goddess of the Madigas. While all castes have much fear of her, and contribute to her worship, caste distinctions prevent any but Madigas from taking an active part in the ceremonies. As the Madigas are usually very poor, her worship is not so extensive or elaborate as that of the other goddesses. She is represented by a small stone image in a very poor shrine.[20]

In preparation for the *jatara* a small buffalo is procured and then turned loose until the appointed day. The image is then

[20] There is an occasional exception. In Kavili, Nellore District, the temple of Mathamma is equal to many small Hindu temples. The Madigas contracted a heavy debt with the Sudras to build it, and this they have not been able to pay, and probably never will pay, the Sudras being satisfied to have the Madigas in their power because of this debt. In Kandukuru also the temple to Mathamma is a large one.

given a bath, a sheep is offered, and there is the usual buffalo sacrifice with the ceremonies already described. On the last day the *pujari,* who is always a Madiga, takes a fowl, cuts off its head before the idol, and, holding it by the legs, brushes away the *muggu,* or sacred marks before the idol, thus removing the last vestiges of the evil which may come from Mathamma.

But Mathamma has another form which is far more important, and this is as a Matangi. A Matangi is a Madiga woman who is supposed to be possessed with the spirit of Mathamma. She is one of the most interesting characters in this Dravidian worship, and later the stories concerning her origin will be given at some length.[21]

The selection of a new Matangi is an important ceremony. The Matangi holds her position for life, and her successor is usually not chosen until after her death. One method of making the choice is to bring all the unmarried girls of the village before the shrine of Mathamma. Songs are then sung, drums are beaten loudly, and the goddess is invoked to descend upon the chosen one. Soon one of the girls will act as if possessed with the spirit, and it is understood that the choice has fallen on her.

There are other ordeals for the new Matangi to pass. The test appears to be that she shall be able to control herself when the possession comes upon her. She is seated on the sacred *muggu* beside a pot of buttermilk, and four other pots of buttermilk are placed around her. Strings are tied from the pots to the roof so close to the girl that if she moves she will spill the buttermilk. Then the possession is invoked. If she passes this test successfully she is invested with the insignia of her position, a basket or sieve, a snake-headed bamboo stick, a bunch of margosa leaves, and a rope with cowrie shells attached.

There are many variations in these ceremonies.[22] At times if a woman simply sits apart and acts strangely, they say the possession is coming upon her and they put her through the tests. In the village of Chendulur the custom is to dig out an ant-hill

[21] See page 97.

[22] E. R. Clough, *While Sewing Sandals,* pp. 62 sq.; E. Thurston, *Castes and Tribes of Southern India,* IV, pp. 303 sq.

3

and seat the girl in the excavation with a basket turned bottom side up over her. The *bavaneedu*[23] then begins the story-telling, relating the deeds of former Matangis. When the possession comes upon the girl she leaps from the ant-hill, tossing the basket aside, and is then acclaimed the chosen Matangi. None of these tests would seem to be very conclusive.

The centre of the Matangi worship is in a village called Malinthapadu, near Cumbum in the Kurnool District. Here every Matangi must come for final initiation. The expenses are heavy, and must be borne by the Matangi or those sending her. There will be much profit to her later by the gifts she receives in the exercise of her office, so the expenses are gladly met.

The initiation is performed by Brahmans, and appears to be simple. The candidates are placed in a row before the goddess Ellamma, who is supposed to be the original form of Mathamma. Their faces are marked with sacred symbols similar to those on the face of the goddess, after which a buffalo is killed as an offering to Ellamma. These ceremonies continue for five days, when the spirit of Ellamma is said to have fully come upon the Matangis. The candidates are then sent away.

One other ceremony is performed usually in the native village of the Matangi. This is some form of a marriage.[24] Usually she is married to a tree, and it is only a matter of form. After that her life knows no moral restrictions.

The Matangi is Mathamma or Ellamma incarnate, and yet it does not appear that she is worshiped. She takes, however, a most important part in the cult of the village gods. If there is no local Matangi, often one is brought from a distance. She marches behind the master of ceremonies in the procession, and when her time comes she becomes possessed by the spirit of

[23] More commonly called *bainedu*. The *asadis* have no part here. There is still another division of the Madiga story-tellers called *kommu vandlu*, horn-blowers. They recite the Shepherds' Purana, but do not infringe on the duties of either *asadis* or *bainedus*.

[24] E. Thurston, *Castes and Tribes of Southern India*, IV, pp. 296, 304, thinks she is not married. This is probably true so far as being married to a man is concerned. E. R. Clough, *While Sewing Sandals*, p. 74, points out that she is married to a tree.

Mathamma. She then runs about among the people, touching them with her stick, spurting toddy from her mouth over them, and backing up against them, all the time uttering strange wild cries. Not only the Madigas, but the higher castes, even Brahmans, stand in line, as anxious to be spat upon and touched by her stick and her person as are the lowest. There is a current story of a rajah who was omitted by the Matangi, she thinking that he was too great for her humiliating ceremonies, but he insisted upon sharing the blessing.

At some parts of the ceremony she speaks things that are well understood. As she rushes about spitting on those who under ordinary circumstances would almost choose death rather than to suffer such pollution from a Madiga, she breaks into wild, exulting songs, telling of the humiliation to which she is subjecting the proud caste people. She also abuses them all thoroughly, and as in the worship of Bangaramma, they appear to expect it and not to be satisfied without a full measure of her invective.

After this ceremony she visits the homes of the Brahmans,[25] and the visit does not appear to be a pleasant one for them. She comes into the courtyard and smears a spot with cow-dung, on which she places her basket. The inmates of the house at once fill the basket with food and cover the top with a layer of powdered rice. Then a small lamp is placed on top of this and lighted. This appears to be the nearest approach to worship the Matangi receives. She then holds out a pot and asks for toddy. Water is usually brought instead and filling her mouth with this she again goes through the process of spattering them all. The women give her their bodices, and the head woman of the house gives her the cloth which she is wearing. The men give her their sacred threads. She then leaves the place, still singing her wild songs telling of the humiliation to which she has reduced the Brahmans.[26]

[25] E. Thurston, *Castes and Tribes of Southern India*, IV, p. 297.

[26] Thurston thinks but few Brahman families now acknowledge this allegiance to Matangi; *Castes and Tribes of Southern India*, IV, p. 297. So far as I can find, Brahmans are loth to acknowledge any connection with the Matangi, but some form of tribute to her seems very general.

RENUKA. Although this goddess is enumerated often as one of the Seven Sisters, she appears to have no separate worship or temple. Her history is much connected with the origins of all the other goddesses, and will be given later.[27]

When other goddesses are named as composing the group of the Seven Sisters, the worship and ceremonies are much the same as that which has been given.[28] None of the ceremonies are without many variations, but the main features are always much the same. The meaning and origin of these rites will be dealt with later.

[27] See page 83.

[28] *The District Manual of Kurnool District,* 150 sq., gives a full account of ceremonies connected with the *jatara* of Peddamma or Sunkalamma. All the ceremonies given in this chapter appear to be present, and also a good deal which belongs to demon and *sakti* worship.

# CHAPTER IV

## Perantalu Worship

A Perantalu is a woman whose husband is still living. She is also described as a lucky woman or a woman who has attained merit. This honorable name is extended to a woman who has been a faithful wife, has borne children, and has died before her husband. When the name is given to a woman who has died, she becomes an object of worship. How this comes about will be described in a later chapter.[1]

The origin of a Perantalu being of a pleasant nature, the worship is usually somewhat milder than that of other similar local deities. The following illustrations will show the character of the worship given to a Perantalu.

In Matsavaram, in the Kandukuru Taluq[2] of the Nellore District, there were at one time two women who were very benevolent, their chief work being the gift of a large irrigation tank to the village. They were mother-in-law and daughter-in-law. After both had died they were called Perantalus, and as such have been worshiped ever since. They are represented by two ungraven stone images over which no temple has been built.

There is a yearly festival for these goddesses, and as in this village there is no famine because of the good tank, the worship takes the form of making votive offerings rather than of propitiation. One peculiar feature is that new clothes are tied upon the idols. These clothes are later appropriated by the *pujari*. Probably because these deities were once human women, this desire for new garments is attributed to them. Many people give these clothes in fulfillment of vows. There is the usual feasting and drawing of decorated carts around the temple. Toward the close of the worship many of the common features of a *jatara* appear. There are blood offerings, but they are not so repellent as in many other cases. A buffalo is beheaded, but the legs are

[1] Chapter VIII, pages 62 sq.

[2] A *taluq* corresponds to a county.

not placed in its mouth, and the head with a light burning on it is simply left as an offering.

The object of this worship appears to be somewhat confused in the minds of the people. It is difficult to see how these benevolent women could have become deities who desire blood offerings. It is probable that the originally simple worship has been added to, and that, without much thought of the nature of these goddesses, the usual exercises for the malevolent deities are performed.

Buchamma is the name of another Perantalu. She enjoys an annual festival lasting three days. Here again we may see a combination of saint-worship and demon-worship. In this case the buffalo sacrifice is omitted, but on the last day of the festival a sheep is killed in front of the image so that it may see the blood flow. This may be from fear that Buchamma, like other village goddesses, has some evil propensities, and so needs propitiation. More probably, as in the case of the worship noted above, this is simply an accretion from the usual Dravidian worship.

In Muppararazuvarepalem, in the Darsi Taluq of the Nellore District, there is a Perantalu called Lingamma, the worship of whom appears to be altogether joyous. There are no blood offerings, even though all castes worship her. The chief object of the worship is to secure offspring, and a marriage ceremony is performed between Lingamma and her husband. Rice is poured over the heads of the images, as is done for the bridal pair at an ordinary wedding, and many offerings are made in fulfillment of vows.

In Pokuru of the Kandukuru Taluq a Perantalu bearing the name Usuramma has risen to the position of the village goddess. She is represented by a rough stone image in a rude temple outside the village. Her worship has become so important, however, that another image of metal has been made for her. The metal image is for use in processions, and is kept by the Brahmans. This shows the influence of Hinduism, for the

Dravidian method would be to make an earthen image for the one occasion only.

Usuramma is a local goddess, and yet she has attained such a great reputation that people come from long distances to worship her. She is a friendly, benevolent deity. She keeps away the evil spirits and gives good crops.

The *pujari* for Usuramma is of the shepherd caste. Every week he brings a simple offering to the temple, and as Usuramma was an industrious woman, and still works for the villagers, her clothes need changing; so he bathes the image, smears it with saffron, and then ties on a clean *koka,* the cloth worn by the women.

Apart from this worship there is informal worship by individuals. When any trouble appears in the village, the women affected by it make vows to Usuramma, which are to be paid if she removes the trouble. The vows are of a pleasing nature, usually being promises to distribute sweetmeats to the children. When such a vow is fulfilled the children are seated in front of the temple; they wash their faces and anoint themselves with saffron, and then receive the sweetmeats.

The annual worship of Usuramma is a more elaborate affair, and as the expenses connected with it are considerable, it is often omitted if all is going well in the village. At least once in three years, however, the great festival takes place.

The great festival usually continues for five days. On the first day there are processions; the temple is circumambulated three times, and all night long the story tellers stir up the people with the tales of the prowess of the olden times. The second day is a day of feasting. This takes place under a sacred *jammi* tree[3] which is thought to be the habitation of spirits and demons. After the feast there is story-telling as before. The third day the processions and story-telling continue. On this day some male member of the priest's family, disguised as a woman, goes about the village impersonating Gangamma, the especial goddess

[3] *Mimosa suma.*

of the shepherd caste. He is proceeded by a Madiga horn-blower, and receives many offerings.

The fourth day the interest increases. All the women who have made vows, fast until the afternoon. Then *kokas* are spread from each house door to the centre of the village, and the women come walking on these, each carrying a platter of well-prepared food called *ugumanchi bhojanam.* After all have come to the place of meeting the drums beat wildly, horns are blown, then the chief story-teller steps forward, and as the noise lulls, his loud chanting may be heard as he tells of the blood-stirring deeds of former days.

The drums beat and the horns blow again, and the people dance in a frenzy of excitement. One of the story-tellers now steps forward and with a large needle pierces the skin of his left side, drawing the thread through. This is the signal for other men who have made this vow to do the same. The crowd then forms into a turbulent procession, and carrying the offerings proceeds to the temple of Usuramma. As the people advance the washermen spread *kokas* for them to walk upon, while a canopy of similar cloths is carried over those who have made vows.

After arriving at the temple they march around it three times, still walking on the cloths. Then coming before the idol, all prostrate themselves and worship it. Those who have made vows come into the temple. The Brahman and shepherd priests take the offerings and after presenting them to the goddess, reserve them for their own use. The cloths are returned to those who have loaned them for the occasion.

In the evening the people of the shepherd caste observe the *domadi,* or marriage feast, in which only married people whose partners are still living may take part. This takes place under the *jammi* tree. Drums are beaten to keep away interfering spirits. The story-tellers, in this case the *kommu vandlu* or horn-blowers, recite the Shepherds' Purana, and at the close of each line the people shout and throw a little food into the air for the spirits and demons.

At the close of this feast a sheep is turned loose and all run

PLATE V

DRAVIDIAN TEMPLES

These temples are always outside a village, and are much neglected except at the times when a *jatara*, or festival, is conducted.

after it. It is the prize of the one who catches it, and the poor sheep is often almost torn to pieces. The common explanation of this part of the exercises is that if the sheep is caught it proves the truth of the goddess. More probably, however, the custom has come down from some ancient shepherd rite. At night the sports continue, people disguising themselves as Giri Razu and Renuka, and acting some of the scenes in the Shepherds' Purana. Some of these stories will be given later.[4]

The fifth day there is still more feasting, then the carts are drawn around the temple. After this occurs the hook-swinging ceremony, which appears to be the only bloody or cruel feature in the entire festival. A goat is tied up to the end of a long pole, which swings horizontally on a pivot at the top of a high post. A heavy stone is tied to the other end of the pole to balance the goat. A man is then tied beneath the goat and both are swung round and round, the man showering down betel leaves on the people. The original method was to swing the man up with the hooks fastened in the flesh of his back.[5] When this was prohibited by the government the hooks were placed in the flesh of a goat's back. This is now also prohibited, and so both are tied to the pole. The placing of the hooks in a goat's back is said to be still very common, and at times the original method of fixing them in a man's back is undoubtedly carried out, if the police are not too near.[6]

In the evening the sports still continue, this time a Madiga being disguised as a warrior. He enacts scenes from the Purana, his chief feat being to cut off a pith post with a sword. After this he leaps and dances about the temple while the shopkeepers

[4] See pages 105 sq.

[5] Ward, *A View of the History, Religion, and Literature of the Hindus*, London, 1818, I, p. 24, tells of hook swinging to Siva. This would make still more certain the Dravidian origin of Siva. See page 12.

[6] See Oppert, *Original Inhabitants of India*, pp. 477, 481. On hook-swinging in Madura District, Mrs. J. S. Chandler sends the following interesting information. "Hook swinging was done in honor of the goddess Mariamman, goddess of smallpox and cholera. The swinging took place in Sholanandan, about twelve miles from Madura, and has not occurred since 1892. In J. S. Chandler's *Seventy-five Years in the Madura*

press him to take presents, hoping thus to secure good luck. And so comes to a close the worship of Usuramma, with its many sports from the olden times, and its slight touch of a severer worship.

*Mission*, page 16, is this paragraph. 'Hook swinging was practised in the first part of the nineteenth century. In 1856 the collector forbade it, but it was revived and stopped two or three times after that. In 1868 it was publicly revived with the consent of the government, and in many places was celebrated by great festivals and vast crowds of spectators. It so happened, however, that in that same year the Governor of Madras, Lord Napier of Merchistown, visited Madura. Mr. Chandler secured the knives and hooks used in the swinging of one of the men, and showed them to His Excellency. This led to the suppression of the practice for the time. The last time it was publicly revived in the District was in the years 1891–2.'

"In the *Madura Gazetteer*, page 324, Mr. Francis speaks of a village by the name of Virapandi where there is a shrine to Mariamman, and adds, '*Ward's Survey* account of 1821 says that in those days hook-swinging took place at this shrine. Another village in the district where the ceremony was once regularly performed is Nallamaram in the Tirumangalam *taluq*. The last swinging occurred there only a dozen years ago.' This book was published in 1906. It is strange that the author did not know about Sholanandan, which was famous for this ceremony.

"Mr. Chandler saw the last hook-swinging. The man did not seem to mind it, and when he was let down said he would go around again if they would give him a present! While the man was swinging, the car on which the swinging pole was erected was dragged around the temple. The ceremony has not taken place since this time. It was performed to get rain, good crops, and general prosperity. The man was chosen by lot, the right to swing being confined to certain families only. Young men only would be selected. It was considered an honor and a privilege to be chosen, and for several months after the swinging the young man received money from bazaar men and others by showing the knife and hooks. He was probably under the influence of liquor when he was swung."

# CHAPTER V

## The Saktis

The word *sakti* is from the Sanskrit, and means energy, force, or power. In Hinduism it is used to express the energy of the gods as manifested in their wives. In this way the wives of the chief Hindu gods have come to be called Saktis. Especially is this name applied to Parvati, wife of Siva.[1]

These wives of the gods receive worship, but there has arisen a definite worship called *sakti puja.* This arises from the Tantras, which are later than the Puranas. The object of the worship is the adoration of the female principle, and its worst orgies are exceedingly loathsome and immoral.[2] These orgies are conducted at night and in secret. Few Hindus would admit that they have anything to do with them, or know anything about *sakti puja.*[3]

There is still a third use of the word *sakti,* and it is with this

[1] W. J. Wilkins, *Hindu Mythology,* Calcutta, 1882, pp. 320 sq. Monier-Williams, *Brahmanism and Hinduism,* London, 1891, pp. 180 sq.

[2] The subject of *sakti puja* is dealt with in all works on Hinduism. For further information see J. Campbell Oman, *The Brahmans, Theists, and Muslims of India,* London, 1909, pp. 26 sq.; W. Ward, *A View of the History, Literature and Religions of the Hindus,* London, 1818, pp. 152, 153, 232–234; H. H. Wilson, *Essays on the Religion of the Hindus,* I, pp. 254–263; W. J. Wilkins, *Modern Hinduism,* Calcutta, 1900, pp. 340 sq.; J. N. Bhattacharjee, *Hindu Castes and Sects,* pp. 407–413; Monier-Williams, *Brahmanism and Hinduism,* London, 1891, Ch. VII, pp. 180 sq.; Dubois, *Hindu Manners, Customs and Ceremonies,* Oxford, 1899, pp. 288–290; J. Fr. Stacker, *The Arsenal,* Madras, 1910, pp. 80, 81; J. Murray Mitchell, *Hinduism, Past and Present,* London, 1897, Ch. IX, pp. 135 sq.; E. R. Clough, *While Sewing Sandals,* New York, 1899, pp. 103 sq.

[3] Monier-Williams, *Brahmanism and Hinduism,* 207, thinks that the worst forms of *sakti puja* are dying out. Oman, *Brahmans, Theists and Muslims,* p. 27, thinks that the rites are practised secretly by a great number of people, especially Brahmans. Shib Chundur Bose, *The Hindus as They Are,* Calcutta, 1883, Appendix D, p. 317, gives a full description of the orgies, which he thinks are not dying out.

form of *sakti* worship that this chapter deals. It is common to call all female Dravidian deities Saktis. It is probable that they have no original connection with the Hindu Saktis, but as they are female deities, this was the easiest classification. The most of them are said to be incarnations of Parvati, the wife of Siva.

While any village goddess is commonly called a Sakti, the term is usually applied to the fiercer ones, and especially to those which have not been incarnated, and have no fixed temple or image. They are really terrible female devils.

The Sakti ceremonies in the Dravidian worship are an entirely different matter from the *sakti puja* of the Tantras. These ceremonies are not markedly immoral, but are far more terrifying than the Sakti ceremonies found in Hinduism. The worship of these Dravidian Saktis is simply propitiation to prevent their doing some evil, as the following illustrations will show.

While the worship of the village deity is proceeding, it is feared that Saktis will be watching, and through jealousy or some other unworthy reason, may do harm, even to the extent of destroying the good that was hoped for from the *jatara*. To prevent any such consequences, the Saktis are propitiated at midnight, after the day when the sacrificial buffalo was killed. An outcast man is brought to the scene of the sacrifice. He smears his body with blood from the beheaded buffalo, winds the intestines around his neck, and takes the liver in his mouth. A pot containing food soaked in blood is placed in his hands, and accompanied by men armed with sticks and old swords, he starts to go to the boundaries of the village.

As this weird procession moves along they shout, *Bali! Bali!* "The sacrifice, the sacrifice," and the people who are in their houses remain in deathlike stillness for fear of the Saktis and evil spirits which are hovering over the procession. The men in the procession shout and flourish their swords and sticks, to keep off these spirits. The man carrying the bloody offering is held up by ropes, and even then often falls to the ground, saying that he sees the spirits. When he thus falls, limes are cut in two and thrown into the air, and lambs are sacrificed on the spot. The man then recovers from his pretended swoon, and the procession goes forward.[4]

After they have arrived at the boundary of the village the bloody rice is left as an offering, and the man who carried it divests himself of his bloody trappings. Often he swoons, or appears to do so, and is carried to the temple of the village goddess, where water is poured over him to revive him. Sometimes the procession, after arriving at the boundary, continues around the village, the bloody rice being scattered to keep out the Saktis.

A variation of this ceremony as reported by Bishop Whitehead,[5] consists in carrying the buffalo head around the village in order to draw a line over which no evil spirit may pass. Any house which has not contributed to the expenses of the worship will be omitted from this protection.[6]

At times individual Saktis are worshiped, the gruesome ceremonies always having the one object of mollifying the anger of the Sakti. Among these Saktis, Kati Ankamma is one of considerable importance. She is the Sakti of the place where the dead are buried or burned, and is feared accordingly. She is said to live on corpses and to kill young children. She also sets fire to houses, and like all other Indian demons, delights in killing cattle.

The worship is by one household, or at times by two or three households in union. It takes place when there has been some unusual trouble which may be attributed to Kati Ankamma. It appears that the household gods are jealous of this worship of

[4] See the account given by Bishop Whitehead, *Madras Government Museum Bulletin*, V, no. 3, p. 131, for some variations. Bishop Whitehead thinks that the man carrying the bloody offering is supposed to be possessed by the spirit of the village goddess. I have been led to believe rather that he is simply carrying the offering to the Saktis, and that he is thus terribly arrayed so that the Saktis will fear to harm him or those with him. See page 125 for a further discussion of this point.

[5] *Madras Government Museum, Bulletin*, V, no. 3, p. 139.

[6] I have seen a farmer going about his field carrying bloody rice, which he scattered as he walked. This too was to keep the demons from his ripening crop. His idea seemed to be that they would be satisfied with the bloody offering when they reached the boundary of his field and so would not injure his grain.

Kati Ankamma, and so they must first be propitiated. Accordingly the day before that set for Kati Ankamma, these gods, such as Dilli Polasi,[7] have their ceremonies.

The household gods are taken to the water in the evening, and kept submerged all night. The next day the *pujari* comes with the musicians, and also with any persons who are possessed by demons, and joining with the worshiping household, they go to the water. After removing the gods from the water they burn incense and sacrifice a sheep. The procession then starts and when the people reach the middle of the village they offer another sheep to the household gods, and when they arrive at the house still another sheep. The gods are then replaced with much ceremony, are smeared with saffron, and worshiped. It is hoped that by these attentions no harm will result from the impending worship of Kati Ankamma.

The next day the worship of Kati Ankamma begins, and is of short duration, for it is not pleasant enough to be extended any longer than is actually necessary. The Madiga story-teller goes to the burial ground accompanied by the people in whose interest the worship is conducted, together with a crowd from the village. The story-teller disguises himself by dressing as a woman, for he has no desire to be recognized later by any of the other deities as the one who did honor to the Sakti. He takes earth and with the help of cotton to make it stick together without unnecessary delay, he hastily makes a rude image. Eggs are placed in the head for eyes, and shells for teeth. The image is dressed with a bodice and *koka,* and glass bangles are placed on the arms.

After preparing the image, food is cooked and a heap of it placed before it. A black goat is brought and killed and its blood is caught and poured into the mouth of the image. This is an unusual proceeding, and shows the terrible nature of the Sakti and its thirst for blood. The image is then worshiped with many prostrations, while the musicians keep up a turbulent drumming

[7] See page 26.

and dancing. But the people soon leave the place, as the ceremonies are not pleasant, and the dangers are many.

As the worshipers return homeward they sacrifice another goat about midway between the burial ground and the village, so that in case Kati Ankamma is not satisfied she will stop for this blood and not follow them into the village. When they come to the house door still another goat is sacrificed, to be doubly secure. The goat sacrificed in the burial ground is given to the story-teller; that sacrificed on the return journey is given to the washerman, who has assisted in the ceremonies; and the owners of the house eat the one sacrificed at the door.

On the next day, in order to make certain that the household gods have not been offended, they are again worshiped. The story-teller comes and makes a sacred *muggu* in five colors before the gods. Over this he spreads a sheet on which he makes offerings of limes, cocoanuts, and various fruits. He sings some story while the musicians keep up a terrible din outside to drive away evil spirits, especially Kati Ankamma. Another goat is sacrificed, and the worship comes to a close.

Donga Sakti is the name of another of these terrible Saktis. *Donga* means thief, and the fact that she is thought to come by stealth and kill the cattle for her own benefit, probably accounts for her name. The worship is at night, for she is believed to be an enemy to gods and men; circumstances which also may account for her sobriquet.

The worship of Donga Sakti is a kind of last resort. After the usual worship of the village goddess, if the trouble or disease does not disappear, the villagers again consult the diviner. Then the possession of Donga Sakti will come upon her and she will say, "You have worshiped your own gods, but are they the only ones that you should worship? You have thrown me away on the boundaries and left me out in the rain, and so now I am bringing these troubles upon you." The people hearing these words are terrified, for Donga Sakti is a demoness not to be trifled with, and money is at once raised for the worship.

The ceremonies take place in the night and are concluded before daylight. Women do not come near, as the danger from evil spirits is great. Among the men only the bravest are present. At the dead of night the potter makes an image in his house. A Brahman comes and performs the ceremonies to induce Donga Sakti to enter the image. A sheep is killed and the blood mixed with rice, which is offered as *naivedyamu,* the oblation presented to Hindu gods.

The idol is then taken in procession through the darkness with flaring and smoking torches. A booth is hastily improvised in the center of the village, and the rest of the night is spent in offering bloody sacrifices, accompanied by the beating of the drums, which does not cease for a moment, but at times lulls while the story-teller recites tales of the acts of the terrible demoness. After offering the sacrifices, food is cooked and placed before the image and another image upon which many offerings are placed is drawn in the dust.

As morning approaches, the procession starts again, this time to the boundaries of the village. A spot is smeared with cow-dung,[8] and on this the *muggu* is drawn with powdered lime. Another sheep is killed and food is again cooked, mixed with blood, and offered to the Sakti. Since every particle of this food must be eaten, all sit down and partake of the bloody meal. When all has been eaten, they turn the face of Donga Sakti away from their village and towards another village, and say, "Amma, now we have done everything for you. Please go away and do not enter our village again." By this time it is nearly morning, and all slip back into the village by devious ways, hoping that Donga Sakti will not follow them and that they will be free from her for a time.

Nadividhi Sakti is another of this group. Her name means "the middle street." The significance appears to be that she comes into the very center of the village to commit her depredations. The method of making the image and inducing her to enter it shows some variations. A booth with two apartments is constructed in the middle of the village. The inner compartment is

[8] Cow-dung is useful in keeping away evil spirits. Probably this idea is the reason for the universal custom in India of smearing the mud floors of the houses with cow-dung and water. The reason usually given is that it is a sanitary measure and it certainly is noticeable that after drying this dressing seems to make the houses fresh and clean.

called the holy place and only the potter enters it. In the outer part stand the priests who are to perform the life-giving ceremony. While the potter is at work within making the image, the priests trace a rude drawing of the image in the dust outside. When the image is finished, it is brought out and placed near this drawing. The drums are beaten at the loudest, and the men yell wildly to keep away interfering spirits. A goat is sacrificed and charms are performed and repeated until it is thought the Sakti has surely consented to enter the image.

In the worship of this Sakti, the household gods are propitiated as in the worship of Kati Ankamma. After this the ceremonies are somewhat the same as those in the worship of village goddesses. There is the buffalo sacrifice, and a large number of sheep and goats are killed. Blood is sprinkled freely over the Sakti, a rite which is not performed with a village goddess. It appears that Nadividhi Sakti is not quite so terrible as some of the other Saktis, and may possibly at some time become a village goddess.

As with most Saktis, the most important part of the worship is the escorting out of the village. In the early morning after the day of sacrifice, before any one has appeared, the potter places the image in a basket after another goat has been sacrificed. The potter carries the basket, and a Madiga, the buffalo head. A few men escort them, waving clubs, and shouting *Bali! Bali!*, while the drums beat as usual. No woman or child dares so much as to look out of the door as the procession passes. To see the procession would mean death, they think.

On the outskirts of the village the procession halts, and the *pujari* makes a harangue to the Sakti. He intercedes for the people, telling her that if she will leave them alone they will worship her faithfully and give her offerings. After repeating *mantrams* and performing charms, the Madiga again takes up the buffalo head and the potter the image. Now only a few of the men follow, the rest going quietly home. When they reach the boundary, they place the image there with her face from the village, put the buffalo head in front of her, and with many protestations of homage, they request her to leave the village.

They then leave her there and go quietly home by roundabout paths.[9]

In some places, in the worship of this Sakti, they bury alive four young pigs at the corners of the village. The pigs are buried with their heads left above ground. Bloody rice is placed in the holes in which the pigs are interred. This is a protection against the Sakti again entering the village.

Lambadi Sakti is the chief goddess of the Lambadis, a wandering tribe of traders well known in South India.[10] The Lambadis are undoubtedly an aboriginal tribe, and their worship is Sakti worship having little connection with Hinduism. It is more like the Dravidian worship, and probably has been adopted from it in part.

When the day for worshiping Lambadi Sakti arrives, they seek the help of the people who usually officiate in the village worship. The potter makes an image in the usual way, and the Madigas have their usual work. The worship consists chiefly of the buffalo sacrifice, with some modifications. When the buffalo is brought before the image, the *pujari* takes the sword, and after telling a story of its divine origin,[11] hands it to the Madiga headsman. The Madiga comes forward to receive the sword, but before taking it he stops and removing his shoes, places the right foot one

[9] *The Gazetteer of Vizagapatam District,* I, p. 75, tells of a curious custom among the Khonds, a hill tribe of Dravidian ancestry which has not yet come into Hinduism. When disease appears among them they prepare a small car on which is placed one grain of saffron-stained rice for each person in the village. Offerings of blood are made, and then the car is drawn to the next village, to deport the demon. The people of the next village pass it on further, and so it is often kept moving for some time. *The Gazetteer of South Arcot,* I, p. 93, tells of a method for removing sickness. A pot is prepared with offerings of saffron, turmeric, etc., and at the dead of night is broken at some cross-road outside the village. This is certainly to lead the Sakti away by one of the roads, or else to prevent her coming into the village. The *Kurnool District Manual,* 1880, Sec. II, p. 152, describes a custom in the worship of Peddamma in which the straw temple is pulled to pieces and scattered so that the demoness will not return.

[10] Thurston (*Castes and Tribes of Southern India,* IV, pp. 207 sq.) gives a full description of these interesting people.

[11] See the note, page 107.

on the left, and *vice versa*. This is in order that the Sakti or any other demon may not be able to recognize his footprints and so follow him later.

After beheading the buffalo they do not place the leg in the mouth, as is the usual custom, but instead remove the heart, lungs, and liver, and place them in the mouth, and smear the head with blood. The image and the hideous head with the vitals in the mouth are afterwards carried to the boundary and left in the usual way.

The Lambadis have another Sakti, called Malayala Sakti, who is the most terrible of all because she requires human sacrifice.[12] She has no image whatever, perhaps for the reason that no one dares to make one for her. The sacrifice of human beings by the Lambadis was reported by the Abbé Dubois nearly one hundred years ago.[13] He says that when the Lambadis wish to make a human sacrifice, they seize the first person whom they meet, and taking him to a lonely spot they bury him up to the neck. They then make a sort of cup from a lump of dough, and place it on his head. This they fill with oil, and placing four wicks in it they light them. All then join hands, and dance around the victim until he expires.

In the village of Pokuru, Nellore District, is a middle-aged man who tells a strange story that corroborates in general what the Abbé Dubois reported. When this man was a boy of five or six years, he was stolen from home by a band of traveling Lambadis,[14]

[12] The Lambadis are not the only people in India who have offered human sacrifices. Max Müller (*Ancient Sanskrit Literature*, Edinburgh, 1860, p. 419) thinks it may have existed among the Aryans. On the other hand, the *Manual of Administration of the Madras Presidency*, I, p. 71, states that human sacrifices were probably very common among the Dravidians, and that the Aryans adopted *sati* and human sacrifices from them. Monier-Williams (*Brahmanism and Hinduism*, p. 24) says that it was probably once part of the Brahmanical system. For further discussion see Crooke, *Things Indian*, p. 262 sq.; E. R. Clough, *While Sewing Sandals*, p. 72; Dubois, *Hindu Manners and Customs*, pp. 652 sq.

[13] *Hindu Manners and Customs*, p. 70.

[14] Thurston (*Castes and Tribes of Southern India*, IV, p. 226) says that the Lambadis purchase children whom they adopt. It is probable that they do purchase children in famine times. But it also seems well established

who took him as far as the Malabar coast in western India. He was stolen for the purpose of sacrifice, and was given into the care of an old woman until he should be of sufficient age. When the boy was ten or twelve years old, the sacrifice was about to be made. But the old woman who had been caring for him had developed a genuine affection for the boy, and while arrangements were being perfected, she warned him of his danger, and helped him to escape. He had lived a roaming life with the Lambadis long enough to be familiar with the forests and the main roads of travel. Secreting himself in the forest by day and traveling by night, he made good his escape, and at last arrived again at his native village.

The account which this man gives of the human sacrifice, which he saw performed, is that it takes place once in three years if a victim can be obtained, but now, since there is more difficulty in securing the victims, not so frequently. He says that they buy or steal a boy from any caste and raise him for the purpose. At the appointed time they select a secret place deep in the forest. The hole is dug, the victim buried, and the lights placed on his head, as described by the Abbé Dubois. A *muggu* is drawn on the ground a little to one side, and on it are placed the various offerings. *Mantrams* are recited to the Sakti, and then the wild cattle-call of the Lambadis rings through the forest. In response all the cattle come running to the place, and trample down victim, *muggu*, and offerings. This ends the ceremony, and immediately they break camp and move on. Fear of detection may be one reason for the sudden removal, but the original idea was probably to leave the region where the Sakti would be likely to remain for a time.

It is a common custom of the Lambadis to bury a pig, leaving the head above ground, when they are about to start on a journey. The cattle are then driven over it and trample the pig to death. This appears to be a survival of the practice of human sacrifice. The same custom of burying pigs alive was noticed above in connection with the worship of Nadividhi Sakti.[15] The similarity in

that they steal children, and that some of these children are secured with the intention of offering them as human sacrifices.

[15] See page 46.

the two rites points to a common origin. It may be that, as the Lambadis have adopted many gods from the Dravidians,[16] they have adopted this custom too, because of the difficulty of obtaining human sacrifices.

Another informant,[17] one of their own number, admits human sacrifice, but says that it has ceased within the past ten or twelve years because of the vigilance of the government. He says that the cattle do not trample the victim, but rush by on either side, while the victim is left to die of starvation unless some passer-by rescues him. A margin of only ten or twelve years since the custom is said to have ceased brings it up practically to the present, and we may well believe that the lonely depths of the forest still witness these terrible scenes, and that this is the end of some of the children whom it is well known that the Lambadis buy or steal, nominally for the purpose of slavery.

Not all Saktis are of so terrible a nature as those described above. Kateri is one of the milder ones. She is said to be a forest goddess who sends cholera and similar diseases.[18] In the Nellore District she is propitiated by pregnant women for a safe and easy delivery. She is said to have a great desire for blood, and the woman fearing that her own blood may be required, makes the propitiation in due time. She is moreover said to be a powerful Sakti who can protect from other Saktis.

This Sakti has no image, but the woman who desires the favor of Kateri takes offerings and also a new *koka,* and calling all the married women of the place, gathers them beside a water pot in a spot previously selected. All the women put on the *botlu,* or sacred marks, and leave with singing and tumult. After they have gone a short distance, the woman who is performing the *puja,* or worship, returns alone. She bathes, offers a fowl to Kateri, cooks the fowl and eats it. She then puts on the *koka* which has been offered to Kateri, and makes various offerings, especially the

[16] Thurston, *Castes and Tribes of Southern India,* IV, p. 230.

[17] A young man who is now studying in one of our schools. When a child he and his smaller brother and sick mother were deserted by the Lambadis when starting on a journey. They were rescued by a missionary.

[18] *Brown's Telugu Dictionary,* Madras, 1903, p. 268.

blood of more fowls. It is very important that she be absolutely alone and that no one see the ceremonies.

Women who have worshiped this Sakti may be recognized by their *kokas*. Kateri appears to be a kind of house-name for a group of Saktis. For Panta Kateri a white *koka* with a black border is worn. For Rakta Kateri, it is a plaid of red and blue, and for Chensu Kateri it is a white *koka* with blue stripes. A woman who vows to this latter one usually takes the name Chensamma.

# CHAPTER VI

## Demon Possession

Every Dravidian god has something of the demon element in it, and the Saktis are pure demons.[1] In close connection with this propitiation of demons is the belief in demon possession.[2] There are many ceremonies performed for the exorcism of these spirits. The following illustrations of exorcism will show the general ideas concerning demon possession.

[1] Brahmanic Hinduism is not lacking in demons. The *Rakshasas* of the Rigveda are demons, and the *Asuras* in the later use of the word are also demons. There is, however, a marked distinction between the demons of Hinduism and the Dravidian demons. For proofs of the origin of Dravidian demon worship prior to and independent of Brahmanism see *Manual of Administration of the Madras Presidency*, I, p. 71. *The State Manual of Travencore*, II, p. 55, also says that demon worship as found among the Dravidians is absolutely unconnected with the higher orders of Hinduism. The most persistent distinction is that the *Rakshasas* and Hindu demons have a divine origin, while the Dravidian demons usually are the spirits of dead people. This will be treated more fully later. There is considerable confusion concerning these two classes of demons, not only in books on Hinduism, but also in the minds of the people. One reason for this is that the Brahmans in their effort to absorb the Dravidian people and religion, have to some extent identified Dravidian demons with their own *Rakshasas*. It is common for writers on Hinduism to treat the Dravidian gods under the heading of Demons or Demonology. More can be learned about them under these headings than under any other given in indexes. On the whole matter see Monier-Williams, *Brahmanism and Hinduism*, London, 1891, Ch. IX; Crooke, *Things Indian*, New York, 1906, pp. 131 sq.; Dubois, *Hindu Manners and Customs*, Oxford, 1899, p. 650; Fausbøll, *Indian Mythology*, pp. 1–41.

[2] The Telugu word for demon is *dayyamu*, for the Sanskrit *daivamu*. The first meaning is a deity or divine being. It has then come to mean spirit of any sort, and as it is the evil spirits which are to be feared and propitiated, in common use *dayyamu* means an evil spirit, or devil. On the distinction between demon and devil see Monier-Williams, *Brahmanism and Hinduism*, London, 1891, p. 231. So far as I have been able to discover, demon possession occurs only in the case of Dravidian demons. The Hindu demons do not appear to take possession of people.

When a person has been sick for a considerable time and other remedies have failed, it is common to call a *bhuta-vaidyadu*, literally a demon doctor. He comes and examines the patient and gives his decision that it is no ordinary sickness, but demon possession. It is necessary for him to know the name of the demon before he can exorcise it, so he requests the people to send for the diviner. The people obey, and prepare an offering of five *seers* of rice,[3] five cocoanuts, five dates, five betel leaves, and some saffron and turmeric. The diviner[4] is then called. She comes, and after various ceremonies and repeating many *mantrams*, the possession of some spirit soon seizes her. The bystanders begin to call over the names of different gods to see which one has entered her. When they reach the name of the household god, the diviner invariably cries out that this is the one. This astonishes the onlookers, who now are thoroughly convinced that the household god has entered the woman. The next thing is for the household god to tell through the diviner who the demon is that is troubling the sick person. After some delay and many contortions caused by the possession, the diviner will usually name some person of the household who has died, saying that his ghost is making the trouble. This ends the work of the diviner, and telling them to call the *bhuta-vaidyadu* again, she departs, taking with her the offerings which have been prepared.

Again the *bhuta-vaidyadu* comes. He makes a *muggu* of magic squares and circles, and in these places stars and numbers. He then asks the sick man to place his finger on any number. He obeys, and the doctor immediately tells the name of the demon which is troubling him. He gives the same name as that given by the diviner, and all are more than ever convinced of the correctness of the diagnosis.

The demon doctor now proceeds with the first part of the exor-

[3] A *seer* is something more than a quart.

[4] The diviner is usually an Erukala woman, sometimes pronounced Yerukala. Thurston (*Castes and Tribes of Southern India*, pp. 438 sq.) gives a full description of these people under the name Korava. See also M. Paupa Rao Naidu, *The Criminal Tribes of India*, No. II, *The History of Korawars, Erukulas or Kiakaries*, pp. 1, 2. They are Dravidians, but because of their nomad disposition have scattered to all parts of India.

cism. Many things are done which appear to have no meaning in themselves, but which by their mysteriousness have a striking effect on the sick man and the bystanders. He takes a thread of seven colors, seven cocoanut shells, seven dates, some leaves, and a pot. Some money must be placed beneath these, and five *seers* of rice poured over them. A goat is sacrificed, or if the people are very poor, a chicken will do. Plenty of *ghee*, or clarified butter, must be furnished, and the women prepare all the offerings for a feast. Meanwhile the amount to be paid to the doctor is decided upon. His fee is large compared with that which other people connected with the village gods receive. An auspicious day for the final ceremonies is selected, and the doctor eats the feast and goes away.

On the selected day the *bhutu-vaidyadu* comes again. He first makes an earthen image of a Sakti. It is made as terrible as possible, and various incantations are employed. A goat is killed, and the blood sprinkled on the image, and the demon doctor goes around the image several times repeating *mantrams*. After a little he sends for the sick man, who comes trembling. As soon as he sees the image he cries out, "Alas, it is this which has taken possession of me for so long!" and falls to the ground. The doctor recites *mantrams* to him, and gives him earth which he must carry to the boundary of the village and throw away, thus getting rid of the demon. It is said that if he is a brave man and has faith in the work of the *bhuta-vaidyadu*, he will recover. Otherwise a greater sickness will come upon him and he will die.

There are different methods of exorcism. Another is as follows. The demon doctor makes three kinds of the sacred *muggu*, and after a bewildering number of small ceremonies he makes an image of dough. He then forms nine small lamps of dough and pours three kinds of oil into them. The lamps are lighted and placed on an offering of food in front of the image. A sheep is sacrificed, its blood caught in a broken pot and mixed with rice. This bloody rice is then sprinkled in the four corners of the room.

The demon doctor now brings a thorn from the *mundlu muvishtu* tree,[5] a rooster's spur, and two or three nails. He dips all these into the blood and pounds them into the ground around the sacred

[5] *Andersonia rohitaka*, Rox. ii. 213. Also called *rohitaka vrukshamu*.

*muggu.* This is to prevent any interference with the ceremonies by an evil eye or by another demon.

After further ceremonies the doctor rubs out the *muggu* with his hand, thus indicating that the demon has been removed. He then places the image of dough, one lamp, and the head of the sheep, in a pot, and the procession starts for the burying ground.[6] Two men carry this pot and two others follow with the pot containing the bloody rice. After reaching the burying ground, they dig a hole and bury both pots with their contents, performing the usual burying ceremonies. After all is over another bloody nail[7] is driven into the earth above the buried pots.

The procession now returns to the house, believing that the demon has been left buried. To be certain that it will not again return, the demon doctor now prepares a charm. After bathing and reciting *mantrams,* he makes a small diagram of nine squares on a a piece of palm leaf. He writes numbers in each square, anoints the whole with saffron, and burns incense before it. He then ties it up with blue and yellow thread into an amulet.

These amulets are very common among the people. Often they are made into a more permanent form, being placed in a small silver cylinder. Almost all village children wear a small silver image of Hanuman, the monkey god, suspended from a cord around the neck, and on each side of the image of Hanuman will be seen one of the small silver cylinders containing the charm.

The above illustrations relate to individual cases of exorcism. In many places, however, exorcism is practiced on a much larger scale. People will come from long distances to consult some renowned demon doctor, or to visit some especially potent place. An illustration of this is found at a temple known as Nattaryan Kovil in the Dharapuram Taluq of the Coimbatore District.[8]

[6] The usual Indian burying ground is simply a piece of waste land outside the village. It is unfrequented except from necessity, as it is supposed to be inhabitated by ghosts. There is no order in the arrangement of the graves, and it is unusual to mark them in any way. Burying is often carelessly done and jackals and other animals disinter the bodies. It is altogether a gruesome place.

[7] Iron is one of the best charms against evil spirits.

[8] The facts here related are taken from an article printed in the *Madras Mail,* June 4, 1912.

In this place there is a temple to the Hindu god, Nattaryan, and also small images and shrines for two deities which are considered to be powerful demons.[9] These demons are thought to have the power to cast out other demons.

Tuesday night is the time when the demons are thought to be ready to give help. The ceremonies continue all night, and well into Wednesday morning. All day Tuesday crowds will be arriving, and by night every available place about the temple yard will be filled with encampments. As darkness comes on the ceremonies for exorcism begin inside the temple yard. The possessed people, with very few exceptions, are women, who have all kinds of nervous troubles, or are epileptics. As many as two or three hundred of these afflicted people may be seen in the temple yard at one time. All surge about and sway backward and forward in every stage of nervous disorder. It is like visiting a madhouse.

In the ceremonies for exorcism, which begin about dark, the priest sprinkles ashes over the prostrate form of each patient to make the demon active. He then rudely tells the demon in the possessed person to wake up. As the priests thus pass from one to another, some one of the patients will begin to sway backward and forward, and then round and round with a counter clockwise motion. Then others take up the same motion, and soon all are swaying round and round. It is a strange phenomenon that all sway in the same direction. Sometimes the swaying is gentle and dreamy, and at other times it is acompanied with loud cries, and at times with reproaches directed at the priests. The afflicted persons often work themselves into a fury and twist violently around, striking the earth with the palms of their hands.

These violent demonstrations indicate that the demon is now active, so the priest comes again and adjures the patient to tell the name of the demon which is afflicting her. One woman gave the name of a young man deceased, whom she had never seen. Another gave the name of a twin sister who had died. The priest now asks the demon if it is willing to leave that night. If the answer is in the affirmative he leads the woman by her hair

[9] Their story is given on page 66.

to a tree about one hundred yards away, and cutting the hair off nails it to the tree. This completes the exorcism.[10]

Sometimes the demon says that it is not going to leave that night, and names another time at which it will leave, perhaps a week or a month later. Then the woman slowly arises and goes away to return at the appointed time. The priests are anxious to get the demons to leave, for they receive four *annas,* eight cents, for each successful case and nothing for the unsuccessful ones. There were about one hundred priests in attendance, mostly Sudras.

The next morning at dawn the observer returned and found a few weary women still swaying to and fro, and still being adjured by the priests to tell the names of the demons. As soon as the sun appeared the work of exorcism ceased, and the whole camp was astir. Large numbers of sheep and goats were brought inside the temple yard and offered to the chief demon god. The heads of the animals were chopped off and placed in a bag for the priest, and the blood poured over the fierce-looking idol. The bodies were handed back to those making the offerings and were taken away to be eaten later. During this ceremony the door of the temple of the Hindu god was closed to prevent him seeing the slaughter. It is reported that from two hundred to five hundred sheep and goats are slaughtered here every Wednesday morning. The priests look like butchers, and the place literally runs with blood.

These offerings are largely the vows which have been promised in case the relief sought is secured. Some of the offerings look to the future and are to propitiate the god so that he will protect the one making the offering from future possession by demons. This method of propitiation with blood shows the direct connection between the Dravidian gods and demon possession. This demon possession is simply one of the activities of the Dravidian deities.[11]

[10] Two trees were covered with hair which had been nailed to them. The trees were overrun with ants and beetles, attracted no doubt by the cocoanut oil so freely used on the hair by Indian women. Both trees were withered from the pounding of so many nails into them.

[11] The *Gazetteer of the Madura District,* I, p. 87, gives another method of exorcism. A stone is placed on the afflicted woman's head. She then rushes away, and when the stone falls it is thought that the demon has gone into the earth at the place where the stone struck. A lock of her hair is then nailed to the nearest tree.

# CHAPTER VII

## Kanaka Durgamma and Poshamma

The descriptions which have been given in the preceding chapters will give a fairly complete idea of the ceremonies in connection with these Dravidian deities. In this chapter the ceremonies connected with two more of the almost unlimited number of these gods will be given. It will be seen that not always are all the ceremonies performed, and that the variations are many. The fundamental principles and ideas of the worship, however, will be seen to be the same.

Kanaka Durgamma.[1] This goddess usually has no regular temple or image, and possesses no fixed festival. She is the Sakti or demoness especially responsible for the welfare of the cattle, and is propitiated when there is cattle disease, and sometimes when there is sickness among the people.

The customary method of beginning this worship is that while the people are considering the steps to be taken to stop the ravages of cattle disease, some woman will suddenly become possessed of the spirit of Kanaka Durgamma, and running to water will throw herself in. The people rush to the rescue and pull her out. She will then run to a margosa tree[2] and breaking off twigs will put them in her mouth as if she were a mad woman.

The people ask the woman who she is, meaning that they wish to know what spirit has taken possession of her. She replies, "I am Kanaka Durgamma, and it is because you have neglected my worship that this sickness has come. I am the one who is killing your cattle." The people now ask what her demands are, and again she replies, "I am Kanaka Durgamma. You have forgotten me. You have not given me offerings of blood. You

[1] I am indebted to F. W. Stait of Udayagiri, Nellore District, for many of the facts relating to the worship of Kanaka Durgamma.

[2] *Ayadirachta indica*, sometimes called the Neem tree. This is a semi-sacred tree. It is held in especially high esteem because its foliage is most luxuriant in the hot season when many trees are bare, and shade is especially appreciated.

have not sent me from your village with honor. So you must build me a temple and offer to me the blood of chickens, sheep, goats, and buffalos. Do me the right honors and I will leave you."

The people, hearing these words, proceed immediately to obey them. The village carpenter makes an image of wood from a branch of a margosa tree. The branch when cut off must not be allowed to touch the ground or it will be defiled. The image is often very rude, but may be more elaborate if the carpenter has some ability. It is usually about two feet tall and represents a woman with a sword in her hand. The carpenter must begin his work in the evening and finish it before dawn. The image when made is placed in water[3] and kept there until wanted for the ceremonies. The Madigas meanwhile make a booth in some convenient grove outside the village. This booth answers for the temple which Kanaka Durgamma demands.

In the morning the village washerman takes the image from the water and after carefully dressing it and adorning it with jewels, he places it on a litter in order that it may be carried in the procession. A great din is kept up with the drums all of the time that the image is being dressed in order to keep away troublesome spirits, and a fowl is sacrificed at every stage of the proceeding.

The image is now carried about the village, the musicians going ahead, and not stopping their tumult for an instant. The procession stops before every house, and the inmates bring out water, often colored red to represent blood, and pour it before the image. Offerings are then made, the chief one being a chicken. The head goes to the headsman, and those who make the offering take the body for the feast later in the day.

It may be ten o'clock or later before all the houses have been thus visited. The image is then taken to the grove and placed in the booth. No fire is to be lighted in the village all day long. It is said that the spirit of Kanaka Durgamma will again go

[3] The reason for placing this and other images in water does not seem to be known by the people. The only explanation which I have been able to secure from the people is that it is for *santi*, which means comfort, quietness, and also propitiation. It is probable that the night in the water is supposed to be pleasing to the goddess, but one Hindu ventured the explanation that it was to cool down her anger!

through the village, and seeing it deserted, will think that all the people are dead and so will be glad to leave.

The exercises in the grove are much like a great picnic. The offerings of the morning are cooked, and a feast is prepared. Each woman brings a double handful of food, and placing incense on it, offers it to the goddess. After the feasting the votive offerings are brought, fowls, sheep, goats, and buffalos.[4] Later there is the procession of carts. There is nothing unduly terrifying in the sacrifices, and there is no Sakti worship. The buffalo sacrifice with the legs placed in the mouth is not made, as a usual thing.

As the day declines the people come one by one before Kanaka Durgamma and bow in worship. They then return quietly to the village. A small procession now takes the image to the boundary and leaves it there, after further sacrifices. By this time it will be dark, and the procession is made with torches. At the boundary these are suddenly extinguished, and the bearers slip hurriedly away in order that she may not follow them.[5]

In Nalgonda in the Deccan, Kanaka Durgamma is not an interloper, but is the village goddess. Her image and temple are permanent, and she is not left on the boundary. In this particular instance a Brahman is *pujari,* but at the time the bloody sacrifices are made he will remain inside the temple so as not to see them.[6]

POSHAMMA. The name means the one who supports or nourishes. The following vivid description[7] presents a good example of the family or private worship of one of these deities.

"I halted my pony in front of several idols that showed signs of recent worship, and began to ask questions about them. Being

[4] At a festival for Kanakama Durgamma in Ramapatnam, Dec. 2, 1912, only one sheep was offered in the grove, and no other animals.

[5] It is evident that the image is not regarded as sacred after the day of worship, for it is not difficult to secure after being left on the boundary. I found one and took it to America in 1909. For a small present I secured the one worshiped at Ramapatnam, Dec. 2, 1912, and have it now in my possession. Mr. Stait also secured an unusually fine one in connection with the worship which he reports.

[6] In this way any goddess may be permanent in one place, and an interloper in another.

[7] For this description I am indebted to Charles Rutherford of Hanumakonda, Deccan.

told that a sacrifice was about to be offered by some of the villagers, I waited and saw the whole ceremony.

"A small procession of a dozen people or so, men, women, and children, came filing out of the village. They were led by a Madiga beating a drum. After him came two men of the washerman caste, each carrying a lamb, and after them came the women, each with a brass *chembu*, or drinking cup, of water, and with baskets containing food and other offerings. The whole procession marched three times around the 'green tree' under which the idols stood, and then halted in front of them. The washerman placed the lambs on the ground in front of the idols. The two women splashed water over the idols, and then bowing low worshiped them. After this they put spots of red, yellow, and purple all over the idols, pressing on the powder with the thumbs of their right hands. This done, each woman placed a small leaf plate of rice before each image, poured *ghee* and curds over the food, and lighted incense. They then worshiped the idols again.

"Next they turned their attention to the sacrificial lambs. These were treated to a splash of water in the face, and colored powder on the nose and forehead, after which they were released for a moment to see if they would shake their heads. Either to get the water out of its ear, or to shake off its recent bondage, one of the lambs shook its head, thus signifying that the goddess was pleased with the sacrifice. The lamb which did not shake its head was promply treated to another splash of water and application of colored powder, when it also shook its head. One of the women explained that this delay was caused by her neglecting to give a promised cloth to the gods, but as she had now renewed the promise the sacrifice had been accepted.

"Since the offerings were now acceptable to the goddess, the washermen each seized a lamb and coolly cutting off the heads, allowed the blood to flow out on the ground in front of the image. Then each severed a forefoot from each lamb and hung them up beside a lot of such feet of various animals which were already dangling in front of the images. This seemed done with the intention that the goddess should not soon forget their offerings.

"When the worship was over the children received the food, the worshipers the mutton, the washermen each a lamb's head, and the poor Madiga received, I am told, about two thirds of a cent for his pains. The reason for this worship was that chicken pox had recently been in the village, and this was a thank offering for protection, or more probably the fulfillment of a vow to be paid if they were protected. Just as I was riding away a young man of the family ran up with the new cloth which had been promised, presented the cloth to the goddess, bowing low before her, and then appropriated the cloth for his own wardrobe."

## CHAPTER VIII

### Local Origins of Dravidian Deities

The great majority of Dravidian deities are of local origin, and in those cases where a local story cannot be secured it is very probable that there was a local origin, the history of which has been lost. In this chapter the local legends of a number of the gods whose worship has been described will be given, together with typical stories of other gods whose worship it is not necessary to describe.

These local stories are of the greatest importance in a study of the Dravidian gods. With no writings and no systems of philosophy or theology, these are practically the only sources from which we may secure any light on the history and development of the worship as well as upon the question of the fundamental reasons for the development of the system.

The legends of the Seven Sisters, while no doubt originally similar to those relating to the other Dravidian gods, have become so much connected with Hindu legends that they will be noticed in Chapter IX in connection with the stories given there. The Perantalu goddesses are always local, and each one has her own story.

The legend of Buchamma[1] is that she was a virtuous woman, the daughter of a man of the *Kamma* branch of the Sudra caste. At one time her husband went to another village on business, and soon a messenger came bringing the tidings that he had died. It was too terrible to believe, so she sent another messenger who returned with the same report. She hurried to her dead husband, and found that the funeral pyre had already been erected. She forbade them burn the body, and then constructed a fire-pit with a structure above it such as the watchers sit on in the fields. On this she placed the body of her husband, and then mounted it herself. She then besought the bystanders to set the wood on fire in the fire-pit.

[1] See page 34.

PLATE VI

DRAVIDIAN DEITIES IN THE MAKING

The couple seated are dead. The woman drowned herself when her husband was dying. Hearing of her act of devotion, he died very happy. This occurred in 1912, but already the names of these dead people are spoken only in whispers, and they are thought to have great powers. It is probable that within another generation the woman will become a Perantalu.

With some protestations they at last consented, and she was consumed with her husband.

Four days later a Mala was passing the fire-pit, and seeing a bit of Buchamma's cloth which had not been burned, he turned it over with the stick in his hand. That night the spirit of Buchamma appeared to her father saying that she had been defiled by this touch and needed to be purified. Her father went to the fire-pit and after searching in the ashes, found her jewels and *tali botu* or wedding symbol. He purified them and kept them in a pot. Soon these relics were thought to have magical powers, and many began to worship them. The worship rapidly expanded; a temple was built; a stone image was made, and Buchamma became a regular village deity.

It is quite probable that this story of the origin of the worship of Buchamma is true. The tendency to deify widows who have performed *sati* is always strong. Her marked devotion to her husband appears to be the characteristic which placed Buchamma in the list of Perantalus.

The story of Lingamma[2] runs as follows. In Mupparazuvaripalem, Darsi Taluq, Nellore District, lived a woman called Lingamma. She was of the Sudra caste, but she and her husband were poor, and worked in the house of a rich man of the same caste. Once some valuables were missing from the house and suspicion pointed to Lingamma. Her employer made her much trouble and was about to take legal proceedings against her, when she ended the matter by jumping into a well and drowning herself.

A few days after this tragic death, troubles began to come to the household of her employer. A little later Lingamma appeared to him in a dream and told him that because of his cruelty she was bringing these troubles upon him. She also threatened him with worse disasters if he did not institute a proper worship for her. His response evidently was not satisfactory, for Lingamma immediately brought a scourge of cholera upon the village and appeared to many as a devil. All were now thoroughly frightened, and led by Lingamma's former employer, they built a temple of

[1] See page 34.

some importance, prepared an image of both Lingamma and her husband, and instituted the worship already described.

We may here see the uncertain state of Perantalu worship. Lingamma was at first considered a devil, and her worship was well on the way to be the same as that of the ordinary demoness. Since, however, she was a faithful wife, dying before her husband, she was placed in the Perantalu category, and the ceremonies show almost no sign of demon worship. As we have seen, it is a time of general merry-making, and of the mildest form of Perantalu worship. Temperamental differences in the worshipers are probably a contributing cause in such variations as this.

The worship of Usuramma[3] has continued for a long time, and the story which accounts for its origin is not very definite. Usuramma was a woman of good deeds who died before her husband. Soon after her death there was an outbreak of sickness in the village. The people addressed themselves to a diviner to learn the cause. She became possessed of a spirit which spoke to the people through the diviner. The spirit said that she was Usuramma, and that she was bringing all this trouble because, while she was worthy to be worshiped, they had entirely neglected her. She instructed them to build her a shrine outside the village where the pounding of the grain and the crowing of the cocks would not disturb her. She promised, if this was done, to come and inhabit the shrine, and that she would then receive their gifts and in return would protect them.

The stories of the local origin of the fiercer Saktis, such as are described above,[4] are not common. Many of these Saktis are demons which do not appear to have been incarnated, and so have no stories. Where stories do exist, the nature of the Saktis and fear of them, would prevent the stories from being popular. An occasional legend is found of the human origin of a Sakti.

Tota Kuramma is a Sakti whose history is told. The story is that at one time there was a great feast in a Hindu house. These Hindus were not Brahmans and had prepared mutton and pork for the feast. While they were eating, a begging Mohammedan

[3] See page 34.

[4] See pp. 40 sq.

and his wife came to the house to ask alms from the guests. The head of the house kindly invited them to come in and eat. They accepted the invitation, and sat down. But the curry which was brought contained pork. Seeing this the beggars were very angry and going out, drowned themselves in a well.

From that time these two Mohammedans have been wandering demons. They go about the villages at night and call, *Kura! Tota kura!* which means vegetables, or commonly simply spinach. If anyone goes out to purchase the vegetables the demons will say, "May your mouth fall," which means, may your speech be paralyzed, and as soon as these words are spoken the one thus cursed falls down and dies.[5]

There is another current story which is somewhat more pleasing. A Mohammedan woman and a Hindu woman were intimate friends. One day the Hindu woman asked the Mohammedan woman to eat with her, and not thinking of the Mohammedan attitude toward pigs, gave her pork curry. The guest recognized the meat, but so great was her love for the Hindu woman that she ate it without comment, and then in shame for her defilement threw herself into a well and was drowned. The Hindu woman, learning what had happened, was fil'ed with sorrow and remorse, and throwing herself into the same well was also drowned. According to this story it is the spirits of these two women who are the demons. The name Tota Kuramma is in the singular number, and appears to be the appellation for the spirit of the Mohammedan woman.

A local variation of this story[6] is to the effect that a Mohammedan woman was found in sin with a washerman. Her relatives, hearing of this, drove her out, and she threw herself into a well and was drowned. Soon after her ghost appeared and played with

[5] It is commonly said that any demon calls three times in the night, so no one responds to a call at night until it has been repeated four times. See *Manual of Administration of Madras Presidency*, p. 81.

[6] This story is current in the Darsi Taluq. It is said that in this region thieves make use of the cry, *Tota kura!* to frighten the people so that they will stay in their houses while the plundering is going on. The people have learned this, and their faith in Tota Kuramma, and fear of her, have much diminished.

the children. When asked its name the ghost replied that she was Tota Kuramma, and gave directions that she must be worshiped.

It does not appear that these demons are worshiped, and they have no image. For protection against them a spot about six inches in diameter on the outer wall near the door, is smeared with yellow earth. On this whitewash is spattered, and on the whitewash are placed the *botlu,* the red marks which are used in Hindu worship. The whitewash represents the Mohammedans, as they commonly decorate their houses in this way, and the *botlu* represent the Hindus. It is commonly said that when the demons pass along the street and see these symbols, they will say, "My big sister is being worshiped in that house, so it is no place for me." That is, they think a stronger demon is there, and so pass on.

The story of the origin of the demons at the Nattaryan temple[7] runs as follows. Years ago a Brahman and a Sudra found themselves together at this place, where there was already a shrine to a jungle demoness called Peycchiammon. As is usual in these stories, there was a woman in the case, and because of her unfaithfulness the Brahman resolved to become a hermit and die there. The Sudra, being his friend, resolved to do the same. They built a small hut and spent the remainder of their lives in peace together. After the death of the hermits some of their followers built two shrines in memory of them, one for the god Nattarayan in honor of the Brahman, and one for the god Virabhadra in honor of the Sudra. Virabhadra,[8] sometimes called Munniyappan, is an incarnation of Siva's anger. Although the temple was built by Hindus, it is evident that the Dravidians adopted this god as one of their local deities, for he is now considered a terrible demon, and is even called *Maha Saitan,* the prince of devils. He and the original Dravidian demoness are the ones who have the power to cast out evil spirits.

The most common story of the origin of Kanaka Durgamma[9] is

[7] See page 55.

[8] See Moor, *Hindu Pantheon,* Madras, 1864, p. 246; also Wilkins, *Hindu Mythology,* Calcutta, 1900, p. 445.

[9] See page 57.

that she was a woman of the Komatie or merchant caste, living near Bezwada. She fell sick and during her illness had a great craving for meat. It was not given to her, and later she died. Soon the cattle in the village began to die, and it was reported that Kanakamma had returned to satisfy her craving for flesh food. She was at once propitiated with blood, and her worship established. The woman's original name was Kanakamma, but as she was considered now to be a Sakti, the name Durgamma was added, and her own name changed to mean "The Golden Durga."

Another quite different story is that there were seven Brahman brothers in a village who had one sister, Kanakamma. Her conduct filled them with suspicions, and when she heard of their state of mind she drowned herself in a well. The people of the village feared a police investigation, and they started the story that Kanakamma had become a Sakti and entered the hills. The spirit of Kanakamma came upon a little girl who spoke for her, and thus the mysterious disappearance of the woman was accounted for.

The story that Kanakamma had become a goddess was not so easily stopped as was the investigation. When the body was taken from the well and buried, the people began to worship at that place, and soon built her a temple. Here her worship is that of a village goddess, and it is when she wanders from this place that she becomes a demon to be carried out of the villages. The word *durgamu* means a hill fortress, and according to this story the name Durgamma was given to Kanakamma because she went to the hills.

Kanaka Durgamma is a very recent goddess. She seems not to have been known a generation ago. It is somewhat remarkable, therefore, that there is not more definiteness regarding her origin. It is probable that the story will assume more definite form as time goes on.

In a village in the western part of the Kandukuru Taluq the household gods in a certain house are a small golden horn and a pair of golden drums. The worship of these is said to be not more than twenty years old. In explanation of the origin of the worship the following story is told.

A Madiga horn-blower, who was a demon worshiper, was a frequent visitor in the village. He knew many *mantrams,* and all the people stood in great fear of him. After a time he established illicit relations with a beautiful caste woman, the daughter of a rich man. The matter became known to the people of the house, but they were unable to do anything to prevent it. Soon the villagers heard of what was going on, and they with the girl's father prepared a plan for the murder of the horn-blower.

When the horn-blower again came to the village, the girl's father called him saying, "There is a devil in my house. A child is sick. The signs are definite. Come and drive out the devil." The man agreed and came to the house. He performed the usual ceremonies, but the demon would not leave. A midnight visit was then planned to the shrine of Poleramma. Taking the usual pots and other articles, he called about twenty people, and they went to the little temple outside the village.

When they arrived at the temple he called for the goat which was to be sacrificed. The people replied that it was ready and would be produced when he had made the preparations. Accordingly he arranged the pots and offerings, drew the *muggu,* made an image of a demon in the dust, and then asked that the goat be brought. Then the people cried out, "You are our goat," and seizing the sword attempted to cut his throat. But no matter how hard they tried the sword would not cut.

The horn-blower feeling that he had been disgraced, and not wanting to live any longer, now said, "O fools, what are you doing? Why are you thus persecuting me? It is impossible for you to kill me. You have satisfied your vengeance, and now I wish to die. There is a knot in my hair. Cut it out and take out the amulet and you will succeed." They did as directed, and two little sticks flew out of the knot of hair. The charm was now gone, and the people killed him, and throwing his body into a hole, trod on it.

The villagers now went to their homes, but their troubles were only beginning. In the morning the village was filled with consternation. Some of the people went mad, and some children and cattle suddenly sickened and died. When the people turned their eyes toward their fields they saw that a blight was already destroying the standing grain.

The afflicted villagers now visited a diviner. She became possessed of a spirit which proved to be that of the dead man who now spoke, accusing them of his murder, and saying that their only relief would be to worship him. But they said, "*Chee,* would we worship a Madiga?" They then went to another diviner, and again to a third, with the same result. Finally the rich man consented and had the horn and drums made and the worship instituted.

This story is rather unusual. It is probably true in its main points, for it happened recently, and is agreed to by all the villagers. These stories are told by the horn-blowers, and the desire of this class of people to instill into the villagers a proper respect for themselves may account for some features of it. It further appears from this tale that male gods are not likely to become village deities. They may be worshiped, but their worship is something outside that which is usually given to the village goddesses. The general interest which the villagers took in this dead man, and the general nature of the disasters which came upon them, would most certainly have created a village deity, had the spirit been that of a woman.

Gonti, a goddess of the Malas, had the more common outcome of becoming a village goddess for this caste. The story runs that there was once a young woman of Sudra birth who lived in the north country. She had brothers but no sisters. She was discovered in sin with a Madiga, and her brothers hearing of it tried to kill her. Gonti fled and hid in the house of the man with whom she had been in improper relations. Soon a young man came to the house. He would have been her brother-in-law according to the new relationship. She failed to arise and show him the respect due a brother-in-law, and when she became aware of her neglect, she fled to the fields, ashamed and also evidently fearing the Madigas.

Some Mala men saw Gonti as she was wandering in the field,

and she told them her story. They promised to protect her, and concealed her during the day beneath a huge heap of straw. When evening came they returned to the village, and taking Gonti with them, they placed her on a beam in the roof of their house in order to conceal her. At night they fastened the door on the outside, but the next morning she was gone and the door had not been opened. Now they were filled with fear, for they believed her to be a goddess, and that they had offended her in some way.

For some unexplained reason the worship of Gonti is connected with the rains. A Mala woman is the *pujari,* and receives many gifts at the time of the ceremonies. When there is famine for lack of rain, an image of Gonti is made and deposited on the boundaries in the usual way. In this respect she has become a Sakti and her presence in the village is not considered desirable.

At the annual festival the ceremonies have a more joyful nature. An image is made of earth and a pot placed over it to conceal it from the Madigas from whom Gonti fled. Dried grass is placed in a grain mortar, and meanwhile the clouds are watched. The ceremony is arranged for a time when rain seems near. When it begins to rain, they say that Gonti has come, and place a pot of milk over the dried grass, which is then ignited. While the fire burns the women sing amorous songs to awaken Gonti, and call her by name. When at last the milk in the pot begins to bubble, they raise a great shout, thinking that Gonti has heard them. After worshiping the image, remembering that Gonti once ran away and probably still wants to do so, they place the image in a basket and after passing it from hand to hand, deposit it on the rubbish heap.

One unusual feature in this story of Gonti is that there is no account of her death. Almost universally it is the ghost of one who has died who returns and becomes the deity.

Podilamma is a goddess of more than usual importance. Her temple is near the village of Podili, a *taluq* town in the Nellore District. She is the tutelary goddess of this town, to which she has given her name. They tell the following story of her origin.

Some Sudra farmers lived in a hamlet at some distance from

the present village of Podili. One day they were treading out the grain with the oxen in a distant field. Their sister was to bring them the midday meal. On the way in a lonely place she met a man. She put down her basket and was late in arriving with the food. When she arrived, her brothers caught her and threw her beneath the feet of the oxen, for they had been watching her while she came, and believed her to be guilty.

The girl evidently killed disappeared under the feet of the cattle among the sheaves. Later when they removed the straw to winnow the grain they did not find the body, but found a stone. A man standing near became possessed with the spirit of the girl and she spoke through him. She said that she had been unjustly killed, and that they must worship her or great evils would follow. All the people who heard this were terrified, and placing the stone in a desirable place they began its worship.

Podilamma, for such was the name of the girl, had now become a deity and soon became noted for power to cure sickness. A rich man who had some serious illness made a vow to her, and was cured. In payment of his vow he had an image made for Podilamma, but it was hideous and all the people feared it. Then another man fulfilled a vow by having a more beautiful image made, and now both images are in the temple. The older image is of stone and has silver eyes which are kept bright, and with a carefully arranged light glare in such a way as to strike terror to the heart of the worshiper. The newer image is of wood and is gaily clothed.

Like Gonti, Podilamma is unusual in that the *pujari* is a woman. The Venkatigiri Rajah, in whose dominions Podili is situated, has given about twelve acres of land for the support of the temple. The offerings are made in the name of the rajah. The *pujari* receives the offerings and lives from them and the income from the land.

The story of Mundla Mudamma is somewhat striking. In a village near Kandukuru lived a little girl of the *Kamma* branch of the Sudra caste, who went daily with the other children to herd the cattle in the waste land which is covered with bushes and small trees. The children often played in the open plain while the cattle were grazing. They played a game in which they knocked small sticks with clubs. It was quite a boys' game, but this little girl, Mundla Mudamma, won every game. The boys made great efforts to win, but with no success.

One day a traveler saw the game, and was filled with wonder, for in India it is not thought possible for a female to have any superiority over a male. While he still watched the children, the cattle strayed into the field of a farmer, who in anger began to drive them to the village pound. The traveler seeing this drew the attention of the children to it, but the little girl called to them that they need not worry about the cattle. She then made a shrill cry and all the cattle came running toward her. The angry farmer tried to gather them together again to drive them to the pound, but all in vain. That night in the village the stranger greatly excited all the people by telling them what he had seen.

The people now watched Mundla Mudamma, and on another day when the cattle had been driven to the pound, she made her cry and they all jumped the walls and came running to her. The villagers now began to fear her, and thought it best to put an end to her activities. There are at least two stories of how this came about. One is that they decided to kill her, but she heard of it and drowned herself in a well. Then her spirit appeared in the village and through a diviner demanded worship.

The other story is that a man who had power with *mantrams* brought it about by his arts that Mundla Mudamma should not be able to pass beyond a certain limited area. She soon discovered the restrictions placed upon her movements, and one day she suddenly vanished, while in her place a black stone appeared. When the people saw this stone they were greatly terrified. They called a workman and after having the stone graven into the form of a woman, they built a temple for it.

The stone appeared at the place where Mundla Mudamma herded the cattle, and it was at this place that the temple was erected. Many people thinking that this was a favored place built their houses there, and a village has grown up which has the same name as the goddess. Like Podilamma, the tutelary goddess appears to have been the founder of the village. Her worship usually lasts for nine days and includes all the characteristic features along with much merry-making.

The story of Ladothamma has some similarities with that of Mundla Mudamma. It contains more pathos than is usually found in these legends. Ladothamma was the little daughter of parents of the *Reddi* branch of the Sudra caste. She was much loved by her parents, but when she was five or six years old she died. A short time afterward when the village children were playing, Ladothamma appeared among them and played with them as she had done before she died. The children told this to Ladothamma's parents, and they came with great eagerness to see her, but while the children saw her day by day, she was never visible to the parents.

At last her parents gave up any hope of seeing Ladothamma again, but they built a temple for her and placed a stone in it. This happened a long time ago, but the worship has steadily increased in importance so that as recently as the year 1912 a new image of the five sacred metals was made for her and fitted over the stone image. This indicates a long step toward the adoption of Ladothamma into the Hindu pantheon.

The unusual feature of the deifying of Ladothamma is that while the ghosts which become deities commonly bring injury to people and cattle, and thus secure worship, there is nothing of the kind connected with this little girl. Even the children did not fear her. Unfortunately, also, not many of the stories are so pure and so pleasing in their nature as this one is. The following story is an example of those which are far more general.

In the Nizam's dominions in the Deccan there lived a Sudra girl named Naganma, who in due time was married to a man of her own caste. Later she had illegitimate relations with a barber, and her husband and brothers drove her from home. She went to her parents, but they would not receive her, so she lived by herself in her native village, Chetty Palem.

At this time a village doctor became infatuated with her. Soon a son was born to her, of whom the barber was the father, but the doctor took both her and her son to his house, and she lived with him. But now the village *kernam,* or clerk, a Brahman, became interested in her. The doctor observed what was taking place, but as the *kernam* is a man of importance and authority, he raised no objections. After some time her relations with the *kernam* became so intimate that he openly took her to his house, where she lived until her death, some ten or fifteen years later.

When the *kernam* took Nagamma to his house he was a poor man, but she was of the farmer caste and immediately took hold of his affairs and handled the servants and farm work so efficiently that soon he became well-to-do. After she died he built a temple for her, and as a sign of especial honor, made an image with his own hands to represent her. As she was particularly interested in agriculture, the temple was built outside the village in the fields. The *kernam* himself became the *pujari,* which no doubt continues to add to his prosperity. The worship is simple, the especial object being for good crops. There are offerings of blood.

This is a very recent goddess, as the death of Nagamma occurred only a few years ago, and the *kernam* is still living. It will be interesting to watch the development of the worship. The unusual feature in the origin of this goddess is that an ordinary Dravidian deity of the village type was established by a Brahman. There appears also to have been no ghost story connected with Nagamma, but her deification was the result of the arbitrary decision of the *kernam.*

Verdatchamma is the name of a goddess whose temple is built on a small island in the great Cumbum irrigation tank. She has a second temple on the bank of the tank. Her story contains the unusual feature of human sacrifice.[10] When she lived on earth as a woman, she and her husband did not dwell together, as she was said to be born of the gods. It is a fact established in history that a nabob gave her a large tract of land. The probable explanation of her acquiring the reputation of having been born of

[10] On human sacrifices in India see note 12, page 47.

the gods is the use she made of her gift. The fact that she did not dwell with her husband indicates an unusual condition in Hindu society, and it is possible that he called her a Sakti because of her unwifely attitude.

Verdatchamma gave the money to construct the great tank which lies between two high hills. There were two chief diggers, probably *maistries,* or foremen of gangs. Every day they dug and every night the bank broke away. The story goes that these two men, who were brothers, then ascended the two hills and discussed the matter, quarreling over it. While they were having this angry discussion a voice came from the ground in the tank. It said, "If you will make a human sacrifice I will stand."

Two shepherd boys named Pedda Kambudu and Chinna Kambudu, heard these words as they were herding their sheep. They reported the words to Verdatchamma, and offered to be the sacrifices themselves. Their only request was that their memory should in some way be perpetuated. The boys were slain, and in their names two pipes were placed in the bank of the tank to discharge the water. The tank was then completed without further trouble.

So runs the story, and there is every reason to believe that the human sacrifice was made. There may be some doubt, however, as to the willingness of the victims. Verdatchamma later built herself a temple on the island in the tank and is said to have died there. The people believing her to be a goddess, built another temple on the tank bank, and erected two stones to the murdered boys. The usual bloody offerings are made at this second temple and before the stones representing the boys.

Such deities rise and fall. Bandlamma is an example of one whose worship is evidently passing away. She appears to be a purely local deity. The word *bandlu* means carts, and she appears to be the goddess of the carts. The story is told that she was originally a goddess in the village of Chandaluru, Nellore District, but one day she followed some carts which were going on the road to Madras. At night they camped at the village of Ravuru, near Ramapatnam. That night she appeared in a dream to one of the cartmen who was a native of that place, and told him that she desired to change her residence, and would protect them if they built her a temple and worshiped her.

Bandlamma soon became a usual village goddess. The outstanding feature of her worship is the hook-swinging ceremony.[11] On the last day of her worship a live goat is swung from a frame placed on a cart, the iron hooks being placed in the flesh of its back. This cart leads the procession. The goat swung from a cart appears intended for the propitiation of the goddess of the carts. It is said that the goat greatly enjoys the experience, and that it bleats with pleasure. Furthermore it does not die, but is turned loose after the ceremony, and comes again of its own accord for the next *jatara!*

The worship of Bandlamma has practically ceased. Only the older people can remember when it took place. The growing sentiment against such cruelties as hook-swinging may have had some influence, and the coming of the railway, which put an end to extensive cart traffic, may have been another cause for the neglect of Bandlamma.

Such are some of the local stories relating to the origins of Dravidian deities. The number of these legends is almost as limitless as the list of the Dravidian gods. The main points in a few additional legends may be given for comparison.

Kitsamma of Gandavarum, Kanigiri Taluq, was a woman who burned herself with her husband. The fact that she spoke from the flames makes her a goddess of unusual power. After her death some of the people who had heard her call from the flames, went to a place at some distance and addressed her three times, to which calls she replied. The configuration of the country indicates that it was an echo which answered.

Kurumayya is a male deity who also owes his origin to an echo. He was the son of a rich man, but after his father died the property was taken by the other relatives. Kurumayya then went to a farmer and hired himself out to herd sheep. One day he fell into a gorge in the hills and died of hunger. When the villagers searched for him they called his name and he replied.

[11] For further information about hook-swinging see pp. 37 sq.

Later they found his body and deified him. At the festival they go to the hills and call and wait for the response.

Mangamma is still another illustration of the same method of making gods. She burned herself with her husband, and after a time a stone appeared on the north side of the village. The people believed that this was Mangamma and built a temple. At the yearly festival they go to the hills and call until she responds. Then knowing that she is present, they proceed with the worship.

Sandamma and Gumpamma were two sisters who did not marry. They had a quarrel and Sandamma threw herself into a cavern in the Velugonda Hills and died there. Her sister then did the same, and the people, saying they were Saktis, began to worship them. The thieves in the hills propitiate them in order to be protected from the police. They steal goats and then cut their throats in front of the images, until blood runs in streams.[12]

Vinukonda Ankamma is a friendly goddess who is said to have been one of seven daughters in a shepherd's house. She was a talkative and somewhat domineering girl. One day she "hid herself," so the villagers say, which evidently means that she died. Soon cholera broke out, and her spirit came upon a diviner and demanded worship. Ankamma is remembered as a jolly village girl, so her spirit does not inspire unusual terror, and her worship is a time of merry-making with but few blood-offerings.

The Akka Devatalu of the fishermen are represented by crude earthen images which stand on a knoll overlooking the sea. Their name means sister gods. There were once several sisters in one house who quarreled and killed one another. Later sickness appeared in the house, and the sisters spoke through a diviner, upbraiding the people because they had not prevented the tragedy of their death. "However," they said, "we are females and so desire worship. If you will worship us you may escape." The fishermen always propitiate these gods before going out to sea. It is possible that the ever restless sea on the western shore

[12] This appears to be connected with sacrifices which the Thugs formerly offered to Kali before going on a thieving and murdering expedition. See Meadows Taylor, *Confessions of a Thug*, London. 1906, pages 26 sq.

6

of the Bay of Bengal, where the tidal waves are always beating, has something to do with the quarrelsome nature of these goddesses.[13]

Kulagollamma is a village goddess of unusual importance in Kavili. Her temple is larger and more imposing than that of many Hindu gods, and is patterned after them.[14] In Sarvaia Palem, near Kavili, there was a *reddi* or farmer, who had a great crop of the grain called *ragi.*[15] One day some one came to buy grain, and the farmer found that no matter how much he measured out, the *ragi* in the bin did not decrease. Wondering what could be the reason he overturned the great wicker grain bin, when a black stone fell out. The diviner was called in, and when the possession came upon her she said, "I am Kulagollamma, the cause of your prosperity. Build me a temple outside the village where I shall not hear the pounding of the grain, and I will stay to bless you. If you do not, I will destroy you and your house and go to another place." This order was obeyed and she has become far renowned. The last great festival was held in September, 1913. The reason given was that the railway which has been built near her temple, gives her the headache, and she contemplates removing to Madras. Thirty-two buffalos were beheaded before her at that time.

Kudullamma is the village goddess of Chakicherala, Kandukuru Taluq. When she is worshiped blood is shed until it flows in streams. Beneath the water pot, to keep it from rolling over, is placed a small ring of grass or wattled twigs called *kudulla.* One night an inmate of a house in this village dreamed that he saw a goddess rise from the *kudulla* under a water pot in his house. She demanded that she be worshiped, and so real was his dream that he secured a stone, said that it was the goddess whom he had seen, and instituted the worship.

[13] There is a sort of taboo connected with these goddesses. The fishermen say that it means death for any one to touch them. A lady was stricken with typhoid fever soon after touching them, and the fishermen attributed her illness to this rashness.

[14] See note 2, page 17.

[15] *Cynosurus coracanus*, a very nutritious chocolate-colored grain.

These are the legends connected with some of the Dravidian deities. It is probable that every Dravidian deity has had a similar local origin but the stories are forgotten in many cases, and the people answer simply that the god was worshiped by their fathers and so they have continued it. This local origin is a definite characteristic distinguishing these gods from those of Hinduism, which originate in the abode of the gods.

In the majority of these local legends the gods were once human beings. This characteristic is so constant that we may suppose that in the cases where a new god appears outright without a human history, there was such a history believed in by those who instituted the worship. They probably simply thought that the history was unknown to them. It is possible also that in the case of these exceptions the influence of Hinduism is shown, for Hindu gods come to the earth with no human mediation.[16]

[16] In Madavaram, Darsi Taluq, there was until recently a god called Potukuri Verabramham, who, while scarcely a village deity, has a most interesting origin. The story as told in the villages where Verabramham is worshiped runs as follows. In a carpenter's family there was a son born who took his place among the other children of the family. When he was a large boy he was one day feeding the cattle, and saw a man who had just died from snake bite. Verabramham, the carpenter's son, at once raised him from the dead. Later some of the villagers were bringing out a dead man to bury him. Verabramham approached the procession and asked what they were doing. Upon being told, he said, "No, he is not dead. He is alive," and immediately the dead man arose and taking up his bier walked away. One day as he was going on a journey a rain came on and he stopped for a short time. After the rain was over it was discovered that no water had fallen near where he had stood. Another day as Verabramham and his disciple were going to Kandipullayyapuram they met a widow who had lost a son, and Verabramham had compassion on her and restored her son to life. Many other such acts are said to have been performed by him.

At last Verabramham died, but on the third day he arose from the grave, and appeared to his disciple and to others. He told them of a coming judgment, of punishment and rewards, and promising to come again in the form of a beggar, he went to heaven and left them.

The followers of Verabramham made an image of him, and the worship has spread to several villages. The worship takes place on Friday, and anyone, irrespective of caste, may officiate. The worship consists in placing various offerings before the idol, but none of the offerings are of blood. Then there are prayers and hymns much after the Christian fashion.

It is not difficult to trace the origin of this god. It is simply an adaptation of some Christian teaching which the founders had heard. E. R. Clough in *While Sewing Sandals*, p. 117, tells of this worship, but none of these stories are mentioned. Many of the first Madigas who became Christians were first worshipers of Verabramham. In 1909, when on tour in the Darsi Taluq with Mr. J. A. Curtis, the priest of Verabramham in Madavaram gave me the image and much of the paraphernalia, and turned the temple into a school house. The image is now in the museum in Rochester Theological Seminary. In a land so hospitable as India to all new ideas, provided they come within the pale of Hinduism, it is surprising that more such gods have not arisen.

# CHAPTER IX

## THE DRAVIDIAN GODS IN HINDU LEGENDS

In addition to the stories of the local origin of Dravidian deities, there are many legends connecting them with the Hindu pantheon. The original legend is usually found in the Puranas, but in every case it has been changed and added to in order that the Dravidian gods may be given a place in it. These are the stories which are told by the horn-blowers and story-tellers at the times of the worship. They are not printed, but often they are written on palm-leaf books.

The origin of these stories in their present form is probably Brahmanic in nearly every instance. They are an effort to connect the gods of the Dravidians with the Hindu pantheon, and are a part of the Hindu plan for the absorption of the Dravidian religion into their own. In some cases, however, there is indication that the Dravidians have seized upon the Hindu story, and by adding some of their own legends to it, have attempted to connect themselves with the higher form of religion and civilization. In this chapter a representative number of these legends will be given.

THE SIVA LEGENDS. The Dravidian gods are more commonly connected with Siva. There is more in the nature of Siva worship that is Dravidian than in Vishnu worship. It is quite probable that Siva himself is an aboriginal god.[1] One of the legends runs as follows.[2]

There were one hundred and one kings ruling over the country of Thiparapuram. They were devotees of Siva, and because of the many offerings which they made, Siva granted them the boons of immortality and of invincibility in battle. Afterwards these kings engaged in many wars, and in every case they were victorious. Finally the people came to Siva and asked him why

[1] For a discussion of this point see pp. 13 sq.

[2] This story is not found in the Puranas.

he had granted favors which gave so much distress. Siva saw his mistake, but could see no way out of the difficulty except to enter the battle himself and try to defeat these kings. He took human form and went to war with the kings, but with the result that he too was defeated and was about to be put to death.

Vishnu Murti, now seeing that Siva was trembling for his life, offered his advice. He said, "At yonder tank the wives of these kings will be bathing at the appointed time. By virtue of their chastity they will make brass pots from the sand, and in these pots bring home water with which to cook the food which gives their husbands such prowess.[3] The chastity of their wives is the reason for the power of the kings, but they have one sorrow; they have no children. You must assume the form of a peepul[4] tree on the bank of the tank, and I will appear as a *rishi*.[5] The women will certainly come to me when they bathe to ask me how they may obtain children. I will advise them to embrace the tree which you will become. You must thus ruin all of these women, and then their husbands will lose their strength."

Siva consented to the plan, and all happened as arranged. After the women had embraced the tree they went as usual to make the pots of sand, but the pots fell to pieces. Again and again they tried, but to no avail. Then in terror they went home and bringing other pots they took water to make food for their husbands as usual. But when the kings ate the food they lost their power and were destroyed by Siva.

After a time all of the one hundred and one wives brought forth children. All were girls. Thinking that Siva was responsible for their being, the children went to him and asked that he would provide them some way to make a living. He directed them to go into the world as Saktis and torment people, who would then propitiate them with food and thus support them. So these Saktis are abroad in the earth, and whenever a new

[3] This test of character is one commonly found in the Puranas. See page 100.

[4] The poplar-leaved fig tree, *Ficus religiosa*.

[5] Otherwise spelled *rusi*. He is a hermit thought to have divine powers.

deity appears, it is simply one of these Saktis assuming a new form.

This legend makes the Saktis to be the daughters of Siva. They are more commonly said to be his wives. This is the relationship established in the following story.[6]

In the older times there was a king named Giri Razu. He had sons, but although he made all kinds of offerings, no daughters were born to him. For a long time he did penance to Siva, and at last Siva's wife, Parvati, had compassion on him and saying that she would be born as a daughter to him, took human form and hid herself in a golden ant-hill near the palace.

That night the king had a dream that a daughter had been born to him in the ant-hill, and so vivid was the dream that in the morning he called his servants and directed them to dig the ant-hill out. After digging they found a golden net such as are now made of ropes to hold offerings before the gods. At the side of this was a *muggu,* and upon the *muggu* a golden lamp. This is said to be the origin of the use of these articles in worship. Beside these sat a maiden, who was Parvati in the form of Sakti with the name Renuka.

The king ordered an elephant to be brought and sacrificed to her. They also brought five hundred cart-loads of cakes, five hundred cart-loads of cooked rice, and five hundred and fifty cart-loads of minor offerings. After presenting these things to Renuka they distributed them to the people who ate them. A golden palanquin was now brought, and placing Renuka in it, the procession started for the palace. After proceeding one foot they stopped, poured out rice, and offered a sheep. This was done at each foot of the journey until finally they arrived at the palace.

Renuka is said to have been changed into one hundred and one Saktis, which have become the village goddesses. In this story the deities are Parvati incarnate, wives of Siva, and so are on an equal footing with Kali. This legend gives a very honorable po-

[6] A story with enough similarity to have suggested this is found in the *Devi Bhagavatam.* It has not been translated into English.

sition to the Saktis, and is an evident attempt to please the Dravidians. The various features of Dravidian worship are represented in the story. The Dravidians have an occasional worship of ant-hills, of which this legend of Renuka may be the origin.

The idea that the goddesses are the wives of Siva is almost universal, and a favorite method of attaching a Dravidian goddess to the Hindu pantheon is by a marriage with Siva or some one of his incarnations. One of the important instances of this is that of the goddess, Minakshi, of Madura.[7]

In the Madura temple[8] is a combination of Siva, Vishnu, and Dravidian worship. The original god was called Chokkalingam, and from his name and attributes we may judge that at first he was one of the local demons. The Brahmans, not wishing to antagonize so important a deity, adopted him into their pantheon. giving him the honor of being an incarnation of Siva.

But there was another powerful local deity, a goddess, who was much more feared by the people than was Chokkalinam, as a Sakti is always more terrible than a male god. Her name was Minakshi.[9] The Brahmans wished to attach this powerful cult also, and accomplished it by arranging a marriage between Minakshi and Chokkalingam, now called Siva.

In memory of this marriage there is a great annual celebration at which often as many as one hundred and fifty thousand people are present. At this celebration the marriage ceremonies are again performed, but they are never completed. While the ceremonies are proceeding, every year without fail some one sneezes at the right moment, and as a sneeze at such a time is most inauspicious, the marriage is declared off for another year. As the revenues of the festival are very large, the real motive of this postponement is to make certain that the festival will be repeated the next year. The sneezing stops the marriage ceremony, but

[7] For the following interesting facts I am indebted to Dr. J. P. Jones, author of *India, Its Life and Thought*, and other important works on India.

[8] This is the third largest temple in the world. It covers thirteen acres.

[9] Minakshi was originally a powerful Pandian queen. After her death she was deified and worshiped by her subjects.

does not stop the drawing of the idol cars and the other excitements of the festival.

Another curious feature of the festival deserves to be recorded. The powerful king, Tirumala Naik, who reigned in Madura two and a half centuries ago, and who built the great palace and much of the temple there, was not a Saivate, but a Vaishnava who also worshiped Minakshi. He devised a plan by which the Saivite and Vaishnava sects should be brought together and at least made to fraternize.

Twelve miles to the north was the temple of the Vaishnava god, Algar, who had himself been a Dravidian god, the local demon of the thief caste, before being adopted into Hinduism. He was said to be the elder brother of Minakshi. The plan devised was to bring Algar every year from his temple to give his sister in marriage to Siva. But he invariably arrives two days late, and disgusted that they did not wait for him he refuses to cross the river or to have anything to do with the wedding. He consents, however, to remain on the other side of the river for two or three days, and it is during this time that the festival reaches its climax. During these days Saivites and Vaishnavas readily mingle together, and unite to raise a considerable sum of money with which to appease the wrath of Algar so that he will go home in peace, and cause no troubles during the year.

The following account[10] of the marriage of Minakshi with Siva shows the Brahmanic interpretation and explanation of the marriage. It may usefully be compared with the description of the actual ceremonies, since it shows the tendency of the Brahmans to provide the necessary Hindu explanation for these ceremonies.

"When the Invincible (Minakshi) was ruling, her foster mother represented to her the propriety of marriage, to which she replied that she would assemble an army and go to fight with the neighboring kings in order to discover among them her destined husband. Accordingly her minister, Sunathi, assembled a

[10] From *Oriental Manuscripts*, translated by Wm. Taylor, Madras, 1835, I, p. 58. The "Marriage of Minakshi with Siva by the name of Sunteras-vara," is translated from the Fifth *Tiruvilliadel* of the *Madura Stalla Purana*.

very large army with which she conquered all the neighboring kings. She next conquered Indren and then proceeded to Kailasa, the abode of Siva, in front of which she was met by Narada, messenger of the gods, whom she forced to retreat. He went and reported the same to Siva, who, smiling a little, arose and came forth. As soon as he appeared, the before-mentioned sign appeared (one of her three breasts withered) at which the amazon being ashamed, dropped her weapon, and the minister said, 'This is your husband.' The god (Siva) told her to return to Madura where he dwelt, and on Monday he would come and marry her; desiring all preparations to be made. All was arranged accordingly, and the gods inferior and superior were present, bringing presents. She was seated beside the god on the marriage throne when Vishnu joined their hands, and afterwards the marriage ceremony was performed amidst the praises and adorations of the *rishis* and others present."

In the great temple at Madura there are two main divisions, one given to the worship of Siva and one to that of Minakshi. The walls of the temple are covered with paintings and other decorations which show the details of the marriage.

THE VISHNU LEGENDS. The legends connecting the Dravidian goddesses with Hindu deities are not confined to tales of Siva. They are also connected with Vishnu. In the Vishnu stories Renuka is the wife of Jamadagni, and to them is born Parasu Rama, or Parasram, one of the incarnations of Vishnu. Renuka is still the source of the Saktis, so these stories make an incarnation of Vishnu to be a son of a Sakti. The story most general among the people runs as follows.[11]

In the midst of a great forest the Rakshasas, the demons of the Vedas,[12] were living upon mountains called Tipurupu Rallu. At this time Dhandigiri Razu was a powerful king. He worshiped all

[11] This story is commonly told during the festival for Usuramma. See page 34. The legend from which it has its origin is in *Sree mad Bagavata*, Madras, 1893, (Sanskrit) *Novama Skandhamu*, pp. 297 sq.

[12] For further descriptions of the Rakshasas see Moor, *The Hindu Pantheon*, Madras, 1864, p. 120; Monier-Williams, *Brahmanism and Hinduism*, London, 1891, pp. 238 sq.

the gods and also the sages and *rishis*, beseeching them to help him overthrow the Rakshasas.

Narada, the messenger of the gods, now came to Dhandigiri Razu and told him that he must either defeat the Rakshasas or cease pursuing them and acknowledge himself defeated. Dhandigiri asked him who would lead the battle against them and he answered, "Your daughter, Renuka, is the person to go." Then Dhandigiri stared into the face of Narada, and said, "Do you think that a great monarch like myself would consent to have a woman lead my battle? Never! I will lead it myself and tear down their ramparts."

Accordingly, Dhandigiri fitted out an expedition and attacked the Rakshasas, but being unable to stand against them, hid in a cave. Renuka learned of her father's plight by means of a vision, and determined to go herself against the Rakshasas and rescue him. She went first to her mother-in-law to secure leave to go, but consent was not given. Her mother-in-law said that she had no desire to help Dhandigiri, even though he was her own brother, and at the same time father of her daughter-in-law,[13] for he had been cruel to her in times past. But she told Renuka that she might ask her own husband, Jamadagni, and that perhaps he would give the desired permission.

Renuka now started on the journey to her husband, who was living far away in a forest, doing penance as a *rishi*. She carried on her head seven pots, in which were rice and water mixed. Her purity was so great that, as she walked along, the water in the pots began to boil without the aid of fire.

As Renuka was going along Vishnu began to talk with Narada about her purity, and at Narada's request Vishnu suggested a plan to destroy her virtue. In accordance with this plan Narada appeared in the way before Renuka as a beggar and asked her for food. She had compassion on him and gave him a little from the pots on her head. A little further on Narada again appeared, this time as a charming little child with rattling ornaments. When Renuka saw the child she burst into merry laughter.

[13] That is, Renuka and her husbands were cousins. This cousin-marriage is a very common and favorite arrangement.

Jamadagni considered that these were wicked acts because he was doing penance, and he determined that his wife must be punished. He thought of his eldest son, and immediately the son stood before him. His father addressed him affectionately, and asked his son what should be done if anyone were found guilty within their premises. "Forgive him thrice," answered the son.

"But suppose the offender commits a sin beyond forgiveness, what would you suggest?" asked the father.

"Why, father, if such a one is found, you must certainly remove his head from his body," answered the son.

"Well, my dear son," said his father, "look now! Your mother is coming. She laughed at that little boy as she came toward our retreat. Do to her according to the judgment which you have pronounced."

"No! no! father," said the son, "I have been nursed by her and I can never do such an atrocious deed with my own hands."

Then Jamadagni was very angry, and said, "Wretch, I will curse you for your failure to keep your word."

"All right, father," replied the son. "I am ready for your curse. Kill me, or turn me into a beggar as suits you, but I will never do this deed."

Jamadagni accordingly cursed his son,[14] and as he saw Renuka drawing nearer he thought of his other son, Parasu Rama, the terror of the world.[15] Parasu Rama immediately stood before his father who repeated the request which he had made to his elder son. This time no objections were raised, and before Parasu Rama had finished making his declaration of willingness to do the deed, his mother stood before him. He drew his sword, and telling her of her fault, he cut off her head. The sword slipped from his hand and went spinning through the air. Parasu Rama cursed his hand for having done such a hideous deed, and immediately the

[14] According to the story in Moor, *Hindu Pantheon*, p. 116, the curse was that his son should be an idiot. In this version of the story four sons were thus cursed.

[15] For information regarding the Parasu Rama avatar of Vishnu, see Wilkins, *Hindu Mythology*, Calcutta, 1882, pp. 162 sq.; Moor, *Hindu Pantheon*, Madras, 1864, pp. 116 sq.

sword fell and severed his outstretched hand, which fell in the dust beside the head of his mother.

Parasu Rama now turned in rage on his father, and accusing him of being the cause of both deeds, demanded that the life of his mother and his own right hand should be restored. "Unless you revive my mother and create a hand to my shoulder you shall live no more," he cried in anger. "Look sharp! I am coming."

Jamadagni seeing that his terrible son was not to be trifled with at once complied with his request, and restored Renuka and the hand. Parasu Rama's hand is now represented by the royal staff and Renuka's head by the snake hood, which are carried at the time of worship.[16]

After Renuka had been brought back to life she upbraided her husband for his act, and then asked his permission to proceed against the Rakshasas that she might release her father. Her husband asked her pardon for causing her to be killed, and then asked, "Who are they against whom you dream of going? Are they not Rakshasas, and so unconquerable? Think of it no more."

"My husband, if you knew my powers you would not speak in such a manner," answered Renuka, "I will show my power provided you can stand the sight without fear."

"What! Am I not a man, a *rishi* who has power to turn a woman to ashes? Do you pretend to think that anything could frighten me?" replied her husband.

"All right," replied Renuka. "Turn your back and do not look toward me until I give you permission."

Jamadagni obeyed, and presently Renuka told him to face about again. He did so and was terrified to see standing before him a Sakti having a thousand hands. In each one of these hands she held a thousand spikes, and upon each spike a thousand bodies were impaled, and beside each one of the impaled bodies was a devil watching, with a torch in his left hand and sword in his right hand.

When Jamadagni saw this terrible figure, all his boasts of bravery were forgotten, and he fled to the underworld. Renuka, fearing that he would never return if he descended, called for him

[16] See page 22.

to come back, but he would not come, so she caught him by the tuft of his hair[17] and drew him up. She then told him that this terrifying figure was Korlapati Ankamma.[18]

Renuka now secured her husband's permission to proceed against the Rakshasas, and she slew large numbers of them, but for every drop of their blood which fell to the ground sixty thousand new Rakshasas arose. Under such conditions victory was impossible. Renuka now thought of her brother, Potu Razu,[19] who immediately stood before her. "My brother," she said, "if you will help me in this trouble I will see to it that you receive a sheep as tall as the sky and a pile of rice as high as a palm tree."

This generous offer induced Potu Razu to promise to do whatever she required. Renuka directed him to spread his tongue over the ground as far as the kingdom of the Rakshasas extended, and not to let one drop of their blood fall to the ground. Thus the propagation of the Rakshasas was stopped and the battle was won. This is the explanation of the offering of a sheep and a pile of rice to Potu Razu whenever the village deity is worshiped.

This legend makes Renuka, the mother of one of Vishnu's avatars, to be the source of the Saktis, and so connects them very directly with the Hindu pantheon. The aboriginal tribes are spoken of as Rakshasas in the Ramayana. It may be that some part of the Dravidian people assisted the Aryans in overcoming such tribes, and that this story, which certainly gives a most honorable place to Dravidian Saktis, was the result.[20]

[17] This tuft of hair, called *juttu* or *tsuttu* in Telugu, is the badge of Hinduism.

[18] This is one form of the Ankamma described on page 24.

[19] See page 24. No one seems to know how it happens that Potu Razu is a brother of Renuka. This legend appears to be lost.

[20] Moor, *The Hindu Pantheon*, Madras, 1864, p. 120. "It is certainly likely that at some remote period, probably not long after the settlement of the Aryan races in the plains of the Ganges, a body of invaders, headed by a bold leader, and aided by the barbarous hill tribes, may have attempted to force their way into India as far as Ceylon. The heroic exploits of the chief would naturally become the theme of songs and ballads, the hero himself would be deified, the wild mountaineers and foresters of the Vindhya and neighboring hills, who assisted him, would be politically converted into monkeys, and the powerful but savage aborigines of the south

A variant of the latter part of the story comes more directly to the matter of the origin of the Saktis. It relates that when Renuka was engaged in her war with the Rakshasas and discovered that from every drop of blood which fell to the ground, sixty thousand new Rakshasas arose, she went in her perplexity to the three gods, Brahma, Vishnu, and Siva. They appeared to her in the form of Brahmans and heard her story. They admitted that the condition was serious, for, if such things continued, the Rakshasas would be so increased that the gods would not be able to live.

The three gods then told Renuka that the solution of the difficulty was to induce the sexless Rakshasas to propagate in the same way that men do. They would then lose their power of unlimited increase; their progeny would be comparatively small; and victory would be easy. Renuka informed them that to bring about such a happy result was not in her power, and they must undertake it.

Still disguised as Brahmans, the gods now took the usual articles and books for reading the horoscope, and went to the abode of the Rakshasas. The Rakshasas saw them and sent one of their number to enquire who were those Brahmans coming to their abode. They sent back the reply, "We are Brahmans, come to read your horoscope, and we can give you much valuable information." The Rakshasas asked what things they could tell, and the Brahmans responded, "We have heard that you have no offspring. If you have offspring you will increase yet more and more." This pleased the Rakshasas and they asked how such a boon could be secured. The Brahmans showed them a tree by the tank and told them to bathe and embrace the tree.

The three gods then became a peepul tree. Siva formed the roots, Vishnu the trunk, and Brahma the branches. One only of the Rakshasas came at first and did as commanded. Upon em-

into many-headed ogres and blood-lapping demons (called Rakshasas). These songs would at first be the property of the Kshatriya or fighting caste whose deeds were celebrated; but the ambitious Brahmans, who aimed at religious and intellectual supremacy, would soon see the policy of collecting the rude ballads, which they could not suppress, and moulding them to their own purposes."

bracing the trunk of the tree, which was Vishnu, it became a female and conceived. She returned and reported to the other Rakshasas and two more came, and later one hundred more. All of these conceived and brought forth children, one hundred and two girls and one boy.

When the chiefs of the Rakshasas heard of this, they ordered that the children should be killed. They were thrown into a well, but the three gods went to the well and drew them out. One could not be found, so there were one hundred and one girls and one boy. They took these to Renuka and told her that the girls should be Saktis who would be set free in the world to get their living by troubling people, but that they should be her servants. The one boy they named Potu Razu, and said that by his help she should overcome the Rakshasas. This she did as above related, Potu Razu preventing the blood from falling to the ground.

This story of embracing the tree is the same that we have met before.[21] Here, however, it is Vishnu who is the trunk of the tree and so the progenitor of the Saktis. Renuka is not so directly connected with the Saktis in this legend, but Potu Razu's origin is accounted for.

The number of Saktis here again is given as one hundred and one. No reason for this number appears to be known by the people. It may be that it is used to indicate indefinite largeness, like the English "one thousand and one."

The original legend of the beheading of Renuka must have arisen from some historical incident, for it is found in the Mahabharata, the Bhagavata Purana, Padma Purana, and Agni Purana.[22] It is also mentioned in the Ramayana[23] as an example of worthy obedience. The story as found in the Puranas relates that when Jamadagni was doing penance in the forest, his family, consisting of Renuka and her four sons, was with him. One day when the sons were away from home, Renuka went to a stream for water. She saw Chitraratha, the prince of Mrittakavata,

[21] See page 82.

[22] E. Moor, *The Hindu Pantheon*, Madras, 1864, pp. 116 sq.; Wilkins, *Hindu Mythology*, Calcutta, 1882, pp. 162 sq.

[23] T. H. Griffith, *The Ramayan of Valmiki*, Benares, 1895, Canto XXI, p. 19.

sporting with his queen in the water. She was envious of their felicity and was defiled by her thoughts. Jamadagni demanded that she should be killed for this, and called his four sons to slay their mother. Three refused and were turned into idiots by their father's curse. The fourth, Parasu Rama, consented. His father was so pleased with his obedience that he asked Parasu Rama to request any boon. He asked that his mother should be restored without any memory of the terrible deed, and that his brothers should have their reason given to them again. He requested for himself that he should be invincible in battle and have length of days. All these requests Jamadagni readily granted.

In this original legend there is no mention of Saktis or Rakshasas. But it was evidently a story which took hold of the imagination of the people, and those wishing to unite the two cults have seized upon it and enlarged it so as to make it belong to both Hindus and Dravidians, and thus form a legendary connection between the gods of the two.

In the *Devi Bhagavatam,*[24] which is a production later than the Puranas, and prepared by the Brahmans to explain the origin of various gods, the story of the Rakshasa embracing the tree is given. Here only the one embraces the tree and she becomes Renuka, and from her arise the other Saktis. This is an interesting variant, as it makes the Saktis originate in the Rakshasas,[25] while at the same time they are the offspring of Vishnu. This attaches them very closely to the Hindu pantheon. At first sight it would seem that there must be some basis for this connection between the Rakshasas and demons of the Vedas and the demons of the Dravidians. Such an explanation is never given by the people, however, and a legend like the above, making this connection, is very rare. The demons of the Vedas and the Dravidian demons have but little in common.

Another legend in which Vishnu is the chief actor, runs as follows. In the beginning there was a Sakti who had amorous desires for Vishnu, and attempted to entice him. Vishnu asked her for her wheel or discus. She gave it to him, and it since

[24] Not translated into English.

[25] On the relation between Rakshasas and Saktis see note 1, page 51.

has become Vishnu's weapon. He then asked her for her eye and she gave him that also. Because she had parted with these things the Sakti "lost one half her fat." Vishnu now told her to go and bathe in the sea to allay her amorous desires, but before she had time to carry out his command, Vishnu drank all the water of the seven seas, and there was none left for her to bathe in.

The Sakti was now very angry, and the gods, Brahma, Vishnu, and Siva, were much frightened, fearing that she would destroy them. From their own bodies they made an image which they named Visva Brahma,[26] and gave life to the image. They ordered him to make them a chariot quickly. When this was ready the gods mounted it and ascended into the skies to be out of reach of the Sakti.

The Sakti wandered over the earth looking for water, and finally found as much as could be put into a cow's track. She poured this water over her head, and returned to where she had left Vishnu. Not finding him she wept, saying that Vishnu had deceived her. Suddenly the three gods appeared above her in the chariot. She saw them and besought them to take her up to them. Vishnu told her to come up to them by the help of the wonder-working discus which he now threw down to her. This she did, but by so doing lost her power as a Sakti. When she approached the chariot she was unable to defend herself, and Vishnu took the discus and cut her into three pieces. Brahma took the trunk, Vishnu the head, and Siva the legs. These three parts became respectively their three wives, Sarasvati, Lakshmi, and Parvati. They then took the blood and with it created one hundred and one Saktis which have in various forms become the village goddesses.

This legend is a direct attempt to attach the Dravidian deities to the Hindu triad. They are the blood and so the life of the Sakti who became the three wives of the gods. The main features of the legend are found in the *Devi Bhagavatam*.

LEGENDS OF KORLAPATI ANKAMMA. In the story of Jamadagni and Renuka, Korlapati Ankamma is the terrible form which Re-

[26] More commonly called Visva Karma or Visva Karmudu. He is the Vulcan of the gods.

nuka assumes.[27] This Ankamma is an important character among Dravidian gods and there are many legends about her. None of these appear at all in the Puranas. They are of later origin, and as Ankamma is the victor and the Brahmans the defeated, it is probable that these stories are of Dravidian origin. They evidently were composed to set forth the humiliation of the Brahmans, a humiliation consisting in their having departed from their traditions to such an extent that they worship Ankamma. Here we may see the modern fear which the Brahmans have of Dravidian devils. The stage is past when the Brahmans goodnaturedly attempted merely to attach the Dravidian goddesses to their own system. Attempting to conquer the Dravidian gods they have been conquered by them, until, although they hesitate to admit it, nearly all Brahmans fear the local deities almost as much as do the Dravidians themselves.

One of the stories is concerning the subjection of seven kings. They were reigning in a certain city, but neglected to worship the Sakti of the place. They even whipped her and threw her away. The *ammavaru*, or Saktis, were very angry over this, and sought for a way to bring these kings into subjection. So the village Sakti took the form of an Erukala woman[28] and went about the village telling fortunes and divining.

Now it happened that the eldest of these kings was sick. When the diviner went to the palace the mother of the sick king asked her to come in and tell about the prospects of his recovery. When the diviner was brought to the side of the sick man he recognized her, and saying that she was not a diviner, but a Sakti, he caused her to be whipped and driven from the city.

Having failed in this effort the Sakti now adopted a Siva disguise, and wearing the *lingam* came to the king. When asked her request she said that it was only a small one. She desired only to be given a great rock in a desert place on which she would plant a flower garden. The king granted her request and she, together with the other Saktis, plowed the rock and planted the garden. When the flowers were in bloom, she brought some to the king,

[27] See page 90.

[28] See the note, page 52.

saying that Siva would be much pleased if the king would use the flowers in his daily worship. The king was much interested, and appointed her to bring him flowers daily.

After a time the woman told the king that it would be more pleasing to Siva if he would come and gather the flowers himself. To this he consented, and for several days came to the garden and picked the flowers. One day, however, the Sakti appeared as a parrot, and pulled the lynch pins out of the king's chariot. She then called, "Thief! Thief!" because the king was taking the flowers. Hearing the cry, all the other Saktis rushed in and binding the king, put him on his chariot, which at once fell to pieces.

The village Sakti now appeared in her usual form and said, "You have not worshiped me, but have driven me out. Nevertheless, if now you will worship me, I will let you go." But the king replied that even though they impaled him on a stick before Ankamma he would not worship the Sakti. The Saktis replied that he had named his own fate. He and his brothers must be impaled on a stake. They cut down a palm tree and made a sharp stake. The kings, however, requested that they might have an iron spike. This point was conceded, and the kings threw themselves on to the spike and were killed. The name of the place was Koralapadu, and so the goddess is called Koralapati Ankamma.[29] This legend accounts for the spikes in the hands of Ankamma, and also for the impaling of animals at the time of her worship. The story then goes on to tell of the complete surrender to Ankamma.

Soon after the death of these kings on the impaling spike, the wife of the head-king brought forth a posthumous son. One day, when he was nearly grown, his companions twitted him with being fatherless. He came in anger to his mother and asked her what truth there was in the taunt. She feared to tell him lest the Saktis should attempt to destroy him also, but he pleaded so strongly that at last she informed him of the manner of his father's death.

Filled with anger the boy determined to destroy the Saktis. He

[29] Koralapati is the genitive case of Koralapadu.

PLATE VII

WORSHIP OF AN ANT HILL

This is a nest of the destructive white ants. It is commonly called an ant-hill. If dug out it is quickly built again by the ants. Cobra snakes are often found in these ant-hills.

THE IMPALING STAKE

The small stone by the stake is Potu Razu. On the stake shown in this picture, the villagers affirm that sheep are not impaled as formerly, but that their legs are tied together and hooked over the stake.

started out, but did not know the way. Seeing a *rishi* at his devotions, he wanted to ask where the Saktis lived, but did not dare disturb such a holy man. He adopted a device, however, to draw the first word from the *rishi.* He placed two stones for a fireplace, and his knee in the place of the third stone. He then placed a pot on the stones and his knee, and lighted the fire in the usual way. When the fire burned his knee, he jerked it away, breaking the pot. After he had done this twice the *rishi* became interested and asked him about his journey, with the result that the boy was properly advised.

The boy went on his journey and came to a flat-roofed house. Ankamma was on the house top. He took out his pipe and played her a tune, and Ankamma danced and danced, and finally came down to where he was. Here the story stops strangely by simply saying that the boy surrendered at once to Ankamma, and agreed to worship her, something which his people have done ever since. The playing of the pipes at the worship of Ankamma is said to be in memory of this event.

The entire legend of Ankamma appears to be a Dravidian composition intended to show the final surrender of the reluctant Brahmans.

LEGENDS OF MATANGI. The stories connected with the Matangi worship are numerous, and throw much light on the effort to connect a worship most decidedly aboriginal with that of the Brahmanic cult.[30] These stories, as will be seen, contain parts of many of the same legends that are applied to other deities. Some of them give evidence of Brahmanic origin, while others evidently arose from the Dravidians. Some of them may now be given.

Brahma had a son, Vasa Devadu, and planned to marry him to Devakka. Before the wedding was celebrated a *rishi* told Devakka's brother that there would be no joy in the wedding; that seven children would be born to them; that if the first lived harm would come to his kingdom, while if the seventh lived the brother's wife would die. Because of this prophecy the brother took a sword, and as all were going to the wedding, attempted to kill his sister. In terror she asked the cause of his murderous intention. He told her of the prophecy, and then she pleaded with him for

[30] See pp. 30 sq. for a description of Matangi ceremonies.

her life, promising to send to him every child as soon as it was born that it might be destroyed. In consideration of this promise the brother consented to the marriage.

When the first child was born it was brought to the brother, but when he saw it he was moved with compassion, and so with all the first six. All were spared. The *rishi* now appeared again and by more dire threats and prophecies so frightened the brother that he set out with all the children on a pilgrimage to Jagannath Swami at Puri. There, when the children were on their faces before the *swami*, he beheaded them all.

When the mother heard of this, she was distracted with grief, but as she had promised to give up the children, she could do nothing. When the seventh child was about to be born, Krishna, knowing of her grief, took the place of the child, and was born to Devakka. Soon, however, Krishna began to fear for himself, and coming to his father, induced him to make an exchange, bringing Papanooka, the newly born daughter of King Nandadu and placing her beside Devakka, while Krishna took the place of the baby girl. Krishna gave as his reason for the exchange that a girl was more likely to be spared than a boy.

Devakka's brother now came to slay that child also. The mother pleaded with him, "Brother, the child is a girl. You must not hurt it. There will be no profit to you if you kill it." But he would not listen, and taking the child threw her into the air to cut off her head as she fell. The girl did not fall, however, but continued to ascend until she stood on the clouds. She then turned and said, "O Kamsada, you are an evil man. You are trying to kill me. I will not destroy you, but my brother (Krishna) is living in another place and he will destroy you." She then disappeared and became the mother of the earth. Krishna now gave order that there should be a light in the world to represent her. The Madigas now claim her as Mathamma or Matangi.[31]

The above story makes Matangi to be the foster sister of

[31] The main points of this story are found originally in the *Sree mad Bagavata,* Decima skandhamu, Madras, 1893, pp. 4 f. The identification of the deified girl with Matangi is a later addition.

Krishna, and so directly connected with Vishnu. A variant of the legend of the origin of Renuka in an ant-hill,[32] makes Matangi to be Parvati incarnate, and so the wife of Siva.[33] According to this variant, Parvati appeared to the king as a beautiful maiden, and when he tried to capture her she evaded him, and disappeared in an ant-hill. The king sent for men to dig out the ant-hill, but the earth was as hard as stone and they made no progress. At last the king grew angry, and struck his spear into the ant-hill, piercing the head of the maiden. When he removed the spear, brains and blood oozed out, and the king and his attendants, seeing this, fell into a swoon.

The maiden now came out of the ant-hill as a great goddess. She held the heavens in her left hand, and the great serpent, Adiseshudu, in her right hand. These are now represented by a basket in the left hand and a stick in the right hand of the Matangi. She also held the sun and moon as plates in her hands, and in one caught the spilt blood and in the other the scattered brains. With the blood she made the *bottu,* or sacred red mark, on the foreheads of the people who were still in a swoon. This is said to be the reason that the Matangi now carries two brass plates containing saffron and turmeric with which she marks the foreheads of the worshipers.

At last the king and his attendants awoke from their swoon, and the goddess now became a maiden again and was taken to the palace. She was afterwards married to the *rishi,* Jamadagni, and became the mother of five sons of whom Parasu Rama was one.[34]

The story is continued in a variant of the legend of the beheading of Renuka.[35] She went for water to the Gundlakamma, a river of the Madras Presidency, and saw in the water the reflection of the great warrior, Karthaviriyarjuna, with one thousand arms, who happened at that moment to be flying across the sky. She

[32] See page 83.

[33] E. R. Clough, *While Sewing Sandals,* New York, 1899. pp. 74 sq.

[34] Thurston (*Castes and Tribes of Southern India,* Madras, 1909, IV, p. 297) gives another variation of the story in which the goddess appeared as a golden parrot and sat on the ant-hill.

[35] See page 88. For still other versions of this popular story see Thurston, *Castes and Tribes of Southern India,* IV, pp. 297, 300–303.

allowed her thoughts to rest on the beautiful warrior for a moment, and then attempted to take home the water by rolling it into a ball, as was her custom. But this time, try as she might, the water would not form a ball, and she was obliged to return home empty-handed.

It was because of this lapse in her chastity that Jamadagni ordered her to be killed. When Parasu Rama shot the arrow which severed his mother's head, it took off also the head of a Madiga slave who was following her.

When Parasu Rama secured the promise from his father that his mother should be reanimated, he went himself to attend to the matter. It was early morning and still dark. He found the head and placed it on the trunk. He then sprinkled holy water on the dismembered body, and it lived. He now saw another head and trunk lying near, and recognizing the face of the slave, he joined the head and body and caused her to live again also.

It was now growing light, and what was his vexation to discover that he had mixed the heads and bodies, and his mother's head was now attached to the body of the Madiga slave, and *vice versa.* He did not dare risk another double murder to put the matter right, and so was compelled to bring the two women to his father, and beg his forgiveness. Jamadagni was angry, but at last consented to accept as his wife the woman who had Renuka's head. He then made the other woman an inferior deity, and she became Matangi.

This surely marks the limit for the mixture of the Brahman and Madiga cults. According to this story Matangi has the body of a Hindu deity and the head of a Madiga woman. It is evidently a definite attempt on the part of the Brahmans to explain the interest which they have in the Matangi, and also an attempt to attach this important goddess to the Hindu pantheon.

Another version of the story[36] relates that Renuka took refuge with the Madigas to escape being slain by her son. When they refused to give her up, he slew them all. When he went later to reanimate his mother he made the mistake of placing her head on the body of a Madiga woman, but no one else was reanimated.

[36] E. R. Clough, *While Sewing Sandals,* New York, 1899, p. 85.

His father refused to accept this woman as his wife and she remained with the Madigas as Ellamma, who is said to be another form of Matangi. This story appears to be the Madiga recension of the former story in which the slave became Matangi.

The *asadis,* Madiga story tellers, recite a legend[37] which gives a still further account of the connection between Matangi and Ellamma, but does not make them identical. According to this tale, Ellamma is the wife of Jamadagni, and so identical with Renuka. She is the original Sakti, and the first cause of the universe. Matangi is an inferior deity who secures her powers by association with Ellamma.

The story proceeds to tell that one day Ellamma was going to a town called Oragallu, and was accompanied by Matangi. On the way Matangi's feet blistered, and she sat down with Ellamma beneath a *margosa* tree. She then asked permission from Ellamma to get some toddy from a toddy drawer. He became angry at her request, evidently because she was a Madiga, and tying her to a date palm tree, beat her and gave her basket and cane to his groom.

Matangi escaped and went to a brother of this man, who treated her kindly. He had sixty bullockloads of toddy and offered some to her. She held a *margosa* shell to receive it. The shell would not contain twenty drops, yet he poured the sixty bullockloads into the shell without being able to fill it. He then brought fresh toddy from some palms near by, and the shell was filled. Matangi blessed him and ordered that in every grove three trees should be left untapped for her.[38] Matangi now returned to Ellamma and they determined to punish the first toddy-drawer. Matangi went to him once more, but this time as a young woman selling cosmetics. He purchased them but upon applying them was immediately attacked with all sorts of terrible diseases. Again Matangi appeared, this time as a diviner, and told him the reason for his affliction, whereupon he became her devoted follower and was healed.

This story gives the reason for her worship. It is the same as

[37] Thurston, *Castes and Tribes of Southern India,* Madras, 1909, IV, pp. 306 sq.

[38] This is still a common custom, but the toddy-drawers leave trees in the names of other goddesses beside Matangi.

the reason for the worship of all Dravidian deities, the fear of disaster. This is probably a story of Madiga origin, as it depicts the victory of Matangi over higher castes. The following story is still more evidently an attempt, from the Dravidian point of view, to account for her worship by higher castes.

In former times there was a Brahman named Vera Kalita Raja. He was a beggar[39] and worshiped Poleramma, an unusual practice for a Brahman. In the course of time six sons were born to this Brahman and his wife. Before the seventh son, Pattadhi Rudra, was born he felt the disgrace of his father being a worshiper of Poleramma, and made a vow that he would never worship any of the *ammavaru*. Accordingly he determined that he would not appear in the world in the usual way, and coming out through his mother's back, he entered a gourd and continued to grow in that.

The gourd grew north and south, and one day it separated itself from the vine and began to roll toward the bazaar. Meanwhile his mother was going to the well, and the rolling gourd struck her feet. As it was a large gourd, she called a cart and took it home thinking that she had secured a prize. After arriving at the house she opened the gourd, and her lost son appeared. Immediately the entire house became the color of gold. Soon the father came from his begging, and did not recognize the house because of its changed appearance. He was about to pass by when his wife called to him, and told him the whole story. Then there was great joy in that house.

After this the villagers wanted to choose a king, and they determined that one should be chosen from among the six sons of the Brahman. The sons quarreled about the honor, and finally the eldest proposed that all should secrete themselves in palm trees. An elephant should be brought, a garland placed on its trunk, and whichever boy should be given the garland by the elephant would be king. The plan was carried out, but the elephant passed by all the palm trees, and going to the house where the seventh son was, put the garland on him. So he became the king.

[39] The profession of begging is as honorable in India as is any other method of making a livelihood. Those who adopt it are usually religious mendicants.

Up to this point the story is evidently of Brahmanic origin, but it now begins to take on the Dravidian aspect. The boy who has been so honored because he refused to worship the *ammavaru*, or Dravidian deities, has to submit at last.

The story now goes on to relate that when the new king assumed his authority he commanded that no one should worship any of the village goddesses on penalty of being driven out of the place. The worship of Poleramma now ceased in the village. At the king's command they took Poleramma and throwing her into a miry pit, caused the elephants to tread her down. There were two leeches in the pit, and they helped Poleramma to escape. She now called to her help Mathamma, who was in the hill of Matanga, and also her brother, Potu Razu. These came at once and their first act was to create three hundred and sixty diseases which they put into a bundle and entrusted to Potu Razu.

In the meantime the new king had fallen sick with a carbuncle, and was at the point of death. His mother was frightened and proposed that they worship the *ammavaru*, but he would not consent, saying that the *ammavaru* were the gods of the Madigas, and should not be worshiped in the village. His mother, however, took an offering and went secretly to Mathamma to make her petition. Mathamma replied that if the prime minister's teeth were changed into shells, his ribs into sticks, his stomach into a pot, and his nerves into wires, her son would live.[40]

King Rudra did not consent to these demands, and so Potu Razu went through the village announcing that the next day there would be a *jatara*. He placed a stone in the middle of the village, and called it Potu Razu for himself. He then opened his bundle of diseases, and immediately people and cattle in great numbers began to die. Mathamma now appeared as a diviner, and when they consulted her, she said that all this evil had come to pass because they had driven Poleramma out, and she announced, "I am Mathamma, born in the hill of Matanga. If people begin to wor-

[40] It is said that this demanded transformation is now represented by the *sithara* used by the singers. The instrument often consists of a pumpkin or rude bowl which looks like a pot, on which with the aid of sticks are strung the wires that give the music. Shells are always attached to the instrument.

ship me, all these troubles will go." King Rudra hearing this, consented with all of his people, to worship the *ammavaru* as they are worshiped by the Madigas, and again the conquerors were conquered.[41]

[41] The name Matanga and the feminine form, Matangi, occur in early Indian literature. See *The Ramayan of Valmiki,* translated by T. H. Griffith, Benares, 1895, pp. 246, 315–319, etc. It is probable that there is no connection between these names in the *Ramayana* and the religious institution of the Matangi, except that the names have a common origin. For an excellent discussion of this question see E. R. Clough, *While Sewing Sandals,* New York, 1899, pp. 73 sq. Mrs. Clough is inclined to connect the names in the *Ramayana* with the present institution of the Matangi.

# CHAPTER X

## The Shepherds' Purana

The stories in the preceding chapter are connected with the gods upon which the outcastes have especial claims, gods which probably originated with them. There is another line of legends belonging especially to the shepherd caste. These legends do not deal primarly with the origin of their gods, but they help to throw light on this question as well as on the motives and objects of Dravidian worship.[1]

The chief goddess of the shepherd caste is Gangamma. She has all the characteristics of the other Dravidian deities, and her origin is certainly not Brahmanic. Her story is much confused. Ganga is the name of the Ganges river, and means originally "water." One explanation commonly given for her worship is that she is the symbol of water, one of the elements essential to life. There seems to be nothing either in her worship or in the stories connected with her to indicate any connection between her and the Ganges river. One of the ancestors of the shepherds was named Ganga Razu, and it seems more likely that the name of the goddess came from him than from the river.

The story of the origin of Gangamma, as commonly told by the shepherds, relates that she was in heaven and came down as a spring of water to bless the earth in the *Kali Yugamu*.[2] She then was born in Madurapuri, in the Madura District. For some reason the king wanted to kill her and so she ascended into the sky, and later hid herself in a cave called Amboji.[3] Here she was found by six thousand shepherds.

[1] The shepherd caste is undoubtedly of Dravidian origin. It is a branch of the Sudra caste. Their legends have not been printed, but are found on palm-leaf books, which are jealously guarded. These legends are commonly called the "Shepherds' Purana." They are of comparatively recent origin.

[2] *Yugamu* means age. The Hindus divide all time into four ages, the *Krita, Treta, Dvapara,* and *Kali yugamus.* The *Kali Yugamu* or iron age is considered to be a time of distress and troubles. It is the present age.

[3] *Ambhojamu* is the Sanskrit term for lotus.

Some time later these shepherds were worshiping Siva, when she interfered with their worship, ruining some of the ceremonies. The shepherds became angry and began to whip her with ropes, but immediately she turned into a stone image. They then began accusing and beating one another, and to this day rope whips are kept as a part of the sacred relics of the goddess. This narrative appears to be a mixture of the legend given in the *Ramayana*[4] of the origin of the Ganges river, and of some local story of the origin of a goddess who was thus rather clumsily attached to Hinduism.

Another legend, apparently quite distinct from this one, is connected with the beginnings of the shepherd caste. There were five brothers who were kings among the shepherds. One of them, Pedda Razu, had a war with another king and was slain in battle. When he was dying, the king who had wounded him, pretending to be moved with compassion, asked him to think of the person whom he loved best. This thought would bring that person to his presence. The victorious king expected Pedda Razu to think of his own son, Katama Razu, and thus there would be an opportunity to kill him too.

Pedda Razu, however, thought of the gods, and immediately they surrounded him and placed a guard about him so that no one might touch his blood or his corpse. They called the Adi Sakti, that is the original Sakti, Gangamma, and asked her to stand on guard. She protested that as the battle was raging she could not do so. They then placed a string in a winnowing fan, and drew it around that part of the battle field so that no enemies or demons might cross it and approach the dead king.

Katama Razu now heard of the death of his father, and coming quickly, won the battle. Gangamma, seeing his powers, at once fell in love with him and wished to marry him. But Katama Razu said, "You are a Sakti. How could such a relation be possible?" She would not accept his refusal and vowed to marry him anyway. Katama Razu now made what he considered to be a condition that it would be impossible to comply with. He

[4] Griffith, *The Ramayan of Valmiki*, Benares, 1895, Canto XXXVI, p. 48.

told her that if she could prevent his crossing the Paleru river on his return from battle, he would marry her.

After a time Katama Razu ended the battle and driving the cattle, the spoils of battle, before him, set out on his return journey. When he reached the Paleru river Gangamma was there. Taking an ox and a heifer she hid them under a rock beside the river, and then sat on a branch of a tree to see what would happen.

After Katama Razu had driven the herd across the river, he counted them and found that two were missing. He returned and searched everywhere, but without success. Gangamma finally appeared, and showing him the animals, took them out from under the rock. She now reminded him of his promise to marry her if she were able to impede his progress. Realizing that he was caught, he told her that if she would be born in the house of his uncle, he would marry her. Gangamma consented, and in this way became incarnated, and is now worshiped as the wife of Katama Razu.

In this legend Gangamma appears as the Adi Sakti, a position usually assigned to Ellamma in the popular folklore. The story is like the most of the local stories in that the goddess is a Sakti who was incarnated as a woman, and is worshiped after her death. It is probable that Gangamma was at first a Perantalu. Katama Razu has also been deified, and is often worshiped in connection with Gangamma.[5]

[5] There are many myths about Katama Razu. In the worship of Gangamma a Madiga cuts off the pith post as described on page 37. The following narrative explains the act. When Katama Razu was reigning in Nellore, he was engaged in a war. His brothers could not come to help him, so he sent for Berunaydu, a Madiga king, who at once fitted out an expedition and came to his relief. All the earth trembled when this doughty king set forth. The gods saw him, and knowing that he was certain to conquer, determined to prevent his progress. They placed a great log across the road, such a log as no one had ever seen before, and one that it was impossible to scale. Berunaydu came to the obstacle, and said, "If I can cross this log it will be a great honor to me in the eyes of Katama Razu, but if I cannot, I must return in disgrace." Saying this, he drew his sword, and with one stroke cut the log in two. His army passed through, and went on to victory. This sword appears to be con-

The shepherds worship *virulu* or heroes. Such personages have many of the characteristics of the village deities, but are not female. They are of Madiga origin. The legend goes on to tell of the origin of their worship.

Chenniah Baludu, a brother of Katama Razu, was having a terrible war with the people of Karamapudi. He sent to Katama Razu for help. Katama Razu was in the midst of a war of his own and could not come, so Chenniah Baludu appealed to the Madigas. They came at once and entered into the battle with great success. At night all the warriors lay down to sleep. In the morning Chenniah Baludu sent his prime minister to call the Madigas to a feast which he had prepared for all without caste distinction.

The prime minister did not wish to call outcastes, so he returned after remaining away a sufficient time, and said that the Madigas were bathing. Again he was sent, and again without going near them he returned and said that they were putting on their *botlu,* or caste marks. Once more he was sent, and this time he reported that they were tying on their clothes. As it was growing late, Chenniah Baludu decided to wait no longer, so, putting their share of the feast at one side, he and his men ate their part.

While Chenniah Baludu and his men were eating, some one came to the Madigas, awakened them, and chided them for their laziness. They rubbed their sleepy eyes, arose, and came to the feast. Chenniah Baladu now saw that he had been deceived by his messenger, and explained the matter to the Madigas, inviting them to eat. They did not accept his explanation, however, and accusing him of making caste distinctions, said they would remain seven days and fight his battles, but they would not touch his food. Chenniah Baludu now became indignant and saying,

nected with the one used in beheading the buffalo sacrifice. Its power is explained as follows. In a previous age Vishnu, seeing that in the *Kali Yugamu* men would need much help, called his goldsmith, Visva Brahma, and giving him a lump of gold told him to make four useful articles with it. This sword was one of the articles. It is to be noticed that the sword was given into the hands of a Madiga.

"If you will not eat my food, you shall not fight my battles," he sent them away.

The Madigas returned to Katama Razu, and when he saw that they had returned without fighting any battles or winning any victories, he was angry, and would not speak to them. The Madigas were filled with chagrin, and saying, "We did not have any part in the battle with Chenniah Baludu, and now we have no part with Katama Razu, so it is better for us to die," they threw their weapons into the air, and baring their breasts were slain by the falling swords and spears. For this brave act they were immediately admitted into the heaven of heroes.

The *viralu* now are thought to dwell in the sacred *jammi* tree.[6] The place is marked by a stone, but the spirits are in the tree, not in the stone. They are propitiated especially at wedding times, no doubt with the idea that the powers of these heroes will appear in the offspring. At such times it is common to kill a sheep and throw the blood into the air for the spirits.

These legends of the shepherds show the influence of their pastoral life, and in general are of a milder nature than the other legends cited. It is noticeable also that there is no evidence of Brahman influence. There is almost no attempt to connect their gods with those of the Brahmans. It is probable that the shepherds, living a more nomadic life, and dwelling much on the pasturing grounds far from the towns and villages, have never come under the influences of Hinduism as have the other Dravidians. The basic principles of Dravidian worship, however, are everywhere evident in their legends and worship.[7]

[6] The reason given by the shepherds for the sacredness of the *jammi* tree is that at one time the shepherd kings wished to conceal their weapons, and coming to a *jammi* tree, asked it to guard them. They found a corpse and removing the skin, placed the weapons in that. This they tied to the trunk of the tree. When anyone came near the tree he saw snakes, scorpions, and devils, but the shepherd kings saw only their weapons. Because of this kind act on the part of the tree, it has since been considered sacred.

[7] For further information about the shepherds see Thurston, *Castes and Tribes of Southern India*, II, pp. 292 sq. under "Golla."

## CHAPTER XI

### INFLUENCE OF DRAVIDIAN DEITIES UPON HINDUISM

How has Hinduism been affected by the impact of this great mass of aboriginal belief which it has attempted to incorporate within itself? Perhaps the most surprising fact is that Hinduism has been influenced so little. Hinduism is composite, and while it contains two great cults, the Brahmanic and the Dravidian, there has been but little change in the ceremonies of either cult. The most marked change is in the attitude of the original Hindus, who at first despising the Dravidian gods, have now come to have a very wholesome fear of them, and to join to some extent in their propitiation.[1]

The ritual of Hinduism, however, has been almost unaffected by the Dravidian gods.[2] The Brahman *pujari* still continues to offer incense to the Brahmanic gods, and the common people care but little whether he attends to his duties or not. Meanwhile, the great mass of the people are paying their devotions to their aboriginal gods with practically no change in the ritual from time

[1] *Census of India*, 1891, I, p. 59. "The devils and tutelary deities that have been described above are believed in by all classes of Hindus, from Brahmans downward. A Brahman, it is true, will not attend the festivals of the village goddess, but if misfortune befall him he will send an offering of grain and fruit, though not any animal sacrifice. . . . The Hindu religion is, in fact, a mixture of Brahman and aboriginal beliefs, and the position which either holds in the religion of any particular caste varies with the position of the caste. Thus among the lowest castes the devils and village deities are almost everything, but even pariahs profess some allegiance to Brahmanism. As we rise in the scale we find Brahmanic influence becoming more and more powerful, but the number of Hindus who are altogether free from demonolatry and put no trust in the village goddesses, must be very small indeed."

*The Gazetteer of South Arcot District*, I, 95, remarks to the same effect, "Individual Brahmans are not above sharing in the festivals of the meanest of the village goddesses, and making vows at their shrines."

[2] Such exceptions as bloody sacrifices at Kalighat are so unusual as to be conspicuous. These exceptions are no doubt not the result of Dravidian influence on Brahmanic rites, but rather the result of Brahmans coming into possession of important Dravidian places of worship.

immemorial, even though their worship has long been nominally a part of Hinduism.

If the influence of the Dravidian deities has been but little in modifying the ceremonies of Hinduism, the counter influence of Brahmanism on Dravidian ceremonies has been even less. The Dravidians have conceded almost everything else to the Brahmans, and give them divine reverence, but in the matter of their own peculiar religion they stand where their ancestors did when they worshiped devils in the gloomy forests at the time of the Aryan invasion. The people have consented to have their worship called by Hindu names, but in nature it is unchanged.

Brahmanism, while practically unchanged as to ritual, has not been uninfluenced by Dravidian ideas. One line of influence is in the matter of forming new deities. The ordinary Hindu deity is the offspring of deities, while the usual Dravidian deity has had a human career as an ordinary person. Hindu deities have their avatars and live on earth, but as divine persons, and not as ordinary human beings. The following stories will show the tendency for Hindu gods also to be formed locally in the same manner as Dravidian gods.

Near the Tettu railway station in the Nellore District is a small hill on the top of which is a little temple to the god, Mala Konda Swami. The worship is purely Hindu, with no evidence that any of the rites for Dravidian gods have ever been performed there. The story of the origin of this god is, however, that of a local Dravidian deity. It runs in this way.

Many years ago a small Brahman boy herded cattle daily in the forest land about Tettu, and commonly drove his cattle to this hill to graze. One day, while playing with the other boys on the hill, he trod on a black stone, and kicked it contemptuously with his foot, rolling it over a few times. That night the boy took his usual bath and went to bed, but soon he was in a high fever, tossing with delirium, and terrifying the entire household. In the morning, however, he was well again, and went as usual with his cattle.

The second night the fever was still higher, and the boy shrieked so loudly that the cattle were frightened and, breaking their tethers, fled into the forest. The people of the household performed all kinds of *mantrams,* but to no avail. Next morning he was well again as before.

The third night the boy had a dream in which a figure appeared to him, and said, "I am Mala Konda Swami. You have kicked me disgracefully. You have done me no honor. You have despised and mistreated me, and so these evils have come upon you. If you arise quickly and give me fitting honors, build me a temple and worship me, you and your household will escape. If you do not do this, you will all be destroyed.

The boy awoke and told his dream, but the people thought it was his delirium. To make certain they called a diviner, and she told the same thing. Now they knew that the boy's dream was a real vision, and going to the hill they found the black stone. It was shaped into the form of an image, a temple was built, and the people began to worship it. The *pujari* was chosen from the household of the afflicted boy.

This story very much resembles those relating to the origin of Dravidian deities. It lacks, however, one essential feature, for the boy himself does not become the deity. The following story shows somewhat more Dravidian influence.

The village of Kogilumpadu possesses a local god with the Hindu name, Narayanaswami. At one time there lived a boy of the same name in this village. One day he went with his friends to the forest to gather sticks for fuel. They soon came to an ant-hill, and Narayanaswami stopped here while his friends left him and went further into the forest. When they returned the boy had disappeared, having gone into the ant-hill. They called him, and he answered them from the ant-hill, saying that he would not come out, and commanding them not to call him any more. The children then took their bundles of sticks and went home.

Narayanaswami's mother at once saw that he had not returned, and learning from the children what had become of him, she hurried to the ant-hill and called him. He replied that he would come out if she would go away, but his mother would not leave.

The boy's father soon joined her, and for three days they waited beside the ant-hill. At the end of that time Narayanaswami came out covered with dirt, and with his hands full of cobra snakes as proof that he had been to the lower world.

The boy now went to the village and walked about the streets, eating nothing, and not going home. He announced that if anyone were bitten by a snake or stung by a scorpion, he should put a stone on his head and coming to the ant-hill call, "Narayanaswami!" Those who did this would be cured. After making this announcement he returned to the ant-hill and disappeared in it, never again to come out. Some time later children in the village began to be possessed with evil spirits, and the diviner announced that it was Narayanaswami who was troubling them. The people then built him a temple and his worship began.

From what other information can be gleaned, it seems probable that the boy died in some uncanny way in the forest. He may have been bitten by a snake from the ant-hill. In the worship there are a few customs connected with the village deities. One sheep only is offered, and the rest of the ceremonies are Hindu in character. All castes worship, from the highest to the lowest. The deity is a male, so their worship is not Sakti worship. The connection with the serpents is Hindu.[3] It seems to be a fairly even mixture of Dravidian and Hindu cult and legend.

Another important instance of the tendency to originate Hindu gods after the fashion of village deities is found in the case of Kotappa Konda Swami near Narsaravupett in the Guntur District.[4] The legend runs that about one hundred years ago a man named Yellamanda Kotiah of the Linga Bulija division of the Sudra caste, ruined the wife of a shepherd when she was herding cattle on the hill. The deed became known to her husband, and he determined to seek revenge. The next day he went himself to herd the cattle, and when Kotiah came, expecting to meet the woman

[3] Fergusson (*Tree and Serpent Worship*, p. 58) says that serpent worship is not Dravidian. See also *Manual of Administration of the Madras Presidency*, I, p. 72.

[4] For the facts relating to this god I am indebted to W. E. Boggs of Sattenapalle, Guntur District.

as usual, her husband fell on him and killed him. He also killed his guilty wife near the same spot.[5]

Soon after this the villagers heard a voice rising from the place where the blood fell. The voice threatened them with destruction if they did not build a temple and institute worship for the murdered man whose blood was crying to them from the ground. The temple was built for Kotiah to whom the name of Kotappa Konda Swami was now given. A shrine was erected to the murdered woman who is now worshiped as a Sakti. The ceremonies connected with the Sakti are, however, unimportant as compared with those of the other deity. His worship is strictly Hindu with no bloody sacrifices.

There is an annual *tirunalla*[6] at which often as many as one hundred thousand people are present. This festival begins on Siva Ratri.[7] The object of the worship is to secure productiveness in both people and cattle. For some weeks prior to the festival the farmers drive their cattle around the hill, and husbands and wives desiring children tie their clothes together and walk around it.

The most characteristic feature of the festival is the number of *prabhas* which are brought to honor the god. A *prabha* is a tall structure of bamboo poles erected on a cart and decorated with fantastic banners and pictures of the gods. In this case some of them reach a height of ninety feet, and it takes much ingenuity to manage them in heavy winds. From all quarters of the land these *prabhas* converge on the hill, accompanied by great crowds of men, women, and children, running and shouting, while bands of music precede them.[8]

[5] Another story is that the man, Kotiah, was a *rishi* who was living in the hill, and that the woman in the case was a shepherd girl who daily brought him buttermilk. She had seven brothers, and when they heard of the sinful relations, they slew them both.

[6] See note 5, page 21.

[7] *Siva Ratri*, meaning Siva's Night, is the most important festival for that god. It usually takes place in February. For a description of the ceremonies see John Murdoch, *Hindu and Muhammadan Festivals,* Madras, 1904, pp. 28 sq.

[8] The offerings at this festival are large. They belong to the ex-zemindar

In the case of Kotappa Konda Swami it seems that a local incident, viz., the murder of a man, has caused him to become a god, whom the Hindus have later adopted as an incarnation of Siva. There is another method of uniting Dravidian and Hindu origins in which the god is first Hindu, and the Dravidian love of local legends has gradually built up a local history. The following instance is an illustration of this method.

In the village of Ulavapadu, Nellore District, lives a rich Sudra widow, named Kotamma, who has built a great temple to Venagopala Swami, and supports a large number of Brahman priests. The worship is Vaishnava.

Although Kotamma is still living, already a strange story of the origin of the temple has arisen among the villagers. It is to the effect that at one time Kotamma had a Brahman cook who did not please her. She drove him away with words that were very humiliating to a Brahman. The cook went to another place and secured work, but Kotamma wrote a letter to his new employers, and caused him to lose that place. The Brahman then wrote the history of the entire matter on a palm leaf, tied it to his waist, and drowned himself in a well.

Kotamma had a son at school in Ongole at this time. Soon he fell sick with fever. Then a demon appeared to him, saying, "I am the Brahman whom your mother killed. Did you think that you could do such a deed and escape? Don't think that you are

of Narsaravupett. They amount to so much that the government levies income tax on them. The festival is a great fair where cattle, and all sorts of produce, and even timber, are bought and sold. One of the evil results of the festival is that because of unsanitary conditions it is very often accompanied by an outbreak of cholera which is scattered far and wide by returning pilgrims. In 1909, at the time of the political unrest in India, a riot broke out at this festival in which the police and every one suspected of being connected with the government were attacked. About twenty people were killed. One police constable was tied up in kaffir corn stalks and burned to death. For these murders one man was hanged, and fourteen others were either imprisoned or transported. After this trouble there was an attempt made to transfer the festival to a hill near Sattenapalle, some fifteen miles away. It was announced that the god had changed his residence, but the effort was a failure, and the old festival at the usual place still continues.

rid of me so easily. I have come to take you for your mother's sin." Soon the son died, and a little later a son-in-law died under similar circumstances. Kotamma was in great fear, and to escape the consequences of her sin, built the temple and began to feed the Brahmans.

It is a fact that Kotamma had some trouble with her cook, and that her son and son-in-law died. The temple was not built for the dead Brahman, but as a work of merit. There is undoubtedly some connection between the misfortunes and her desire to pacify the gods. It will be interesting to watch this case. It is probable that the story will grow, and perhaps in time the temple will be said to have been built for the dead Brahman. There seems to be an innate desire in the Dravidian people to have a local legend about their gods.

The legend of Aranjothi[9] involves apparently the adoption of a Dravidian goddess by the Brahmans. The story commonly known among the people runs thus. There was once a woman of high birth who married, but remained with her parents. One night her husband came unannounced and lay down beside her. She did not recognize him and kicked him. Her husband then cursed her and said that she should be born a Madiga. When her father heard of the matter, he called a great council of kings, and as a result the son-in-law was cursed because he had not recognized the virtuous act of his wife. The curse pronounced was that he should be born as the son of a prostitute.

In process of time the two curses were fulfilled. Aranjothi was born a Madiga woman. At that time there was a *guruvu* named Visva Brahma. His worshipers came to him and said, "You are always away on your pilgrimages, so make us an image of yourself which we may worship when you are not here." He agreed, and a five-faced image was made. It was decided that the image must have a wife, so a prostitute was brought and placed before it. By continually looking at her the image caused her to bear a son. This boy was the reincarnated husband of Aranjothi.

[9] Sometimes written Aranzodi, Sanskrit Arundhati.

The people now told the boy that it was proper for one of such birth to go to heaven. He replied that he would not go unless they worshiped him. They said that if he would take sand for rice, and small pieces of iron for *puppu,* and making curry from these, would eat the food from the tiny *jammi* leaf, they would worship him.

The boy took the sand and iron and traversed the entire earth attempting to find a woman who could fulfill the seemingly impossible conditions. At last he came to the Madiga hamlet where Aranjothi lived. She was at that time worshiping Siva. She heard his request and performed the feat. From the sand and iron she prepared a good rice and curry, serving it on the *jammi* leaves which she had deftly woven together.

The man now asked Aranjothi to marry him. She replied that she was a Madiga and he a Brahman, and she was not worthy to marry him. He did not accept her refusal, and declining to leave the house, lay down in the veranda. When Aranjothi's brothers came home they dragged him away, throwing him into a pit, and themselves lay down in the veranda. Aranjothi now realized who her suitor was and married him against the wishes of her people.

Aranjothi's father was now very angry and cursed her, saying that she should be a star in the northeast. When she asked him if he did not have a blessing also for her, he replied that after two ages the *Kali yugamu* would come, and then all would worship her. He then cursed the husband of Aranjothi also, saying that he should become a star in the southeast, but in compensation he was to be known as a *rishi* and worshiped also. His worship, however, does not seem to be continued among the people. Aranjothi now in turn cursed the Madigas, saying that they should always live in poverty, ignorance, and slavery.[10]

Aranjothi can hardly be called a Dravidian deity, as she has no image, but the legend has much to indicate that she is of Dravidian origin. The Brahmans claim that this story is a fabrication made by those who wanted to steal their goddess. On the

[10] E. R. Clough (*While Sewing Sandals,* pp. 53 sq.) gives a somewhat different story, and describes the worship.

other hand, they do not deny the truth of the tale, although they turn their backs when it is told. This story reveals no tendency in the Hindu gods to come down to the Dravidian conceptions, but rather for the local gods to climb up into the Hindu pantheon. We may conclude, therefore, that Aranjothi was once a Dravidian goddess who has been adopted by the Hindus. The name, Aranjothi, is Dravidian, while the Brahmans call her by her Sanskrit name, Arundhati.

Another result of the impact of Dravidian worship is that occasionally Brahmans serve as *pujaris* for the village goddesses. This is rather unusual, and this degradation of Brahmans is not always easily accounted for. An illustration is found among the Togata caste of weavers of Nandavaram in the Kurnool District. These people worship a goddess, named Chandesvari, and even though the offerings are of blood, the *pujaris* are Brahmans.

The story commonly told to show the origin of this strange arrangement is that a South Indian king went with his wife on a pilgrimage to Benares. Unwittingly he incurred a terrible pollution. He applied to the Brahmans to cure him, promising them one-half of his kingdom if they were successful. They asked surety and he called upon a local goddess, Chandesvari, who had a temple near the place, to be his witness. The Brahmans then cured him and he returned to South India.

After a time the Brahmans came south to claim the half of the kingdom which he had promised, but the king denied ever having made such a promise. They then asked Chandesvari to come and give witness for them. She promised to do so on condition that they should walk ahead and not look back at her. The Brahmans agreed and set forth. All went well until they got as far as Nandavaram, when the curiosity of the Brahmans got the better of them and they looked behind them. Chandesvari immediately became an image of stone. The Brahmans were terrified, and built her a temple. Fearing to return to Benares they remained at Nandavaram as *pujaris* for Chandesvari.

It is difficult to solve the enigma of this story. The goddess is one of the ordinary village deities with the usual bloody sacrifices.

It is evident that at some time, against their own wishes, the Brahmans took up the unpleasant task of being priests to a Dravidian demoness. As in nearly all cases of connection with these gods, some great fear of a malevolent deity was the cause.

The Matangi worship also has taken hold of the Brahmans in some places. This is most noticeable in the Cumbum Taluq of the Kurnool District where this worship originated.[11] Here the Brahmans have their own image of Mathamma which they worship. In explanation the Brahmans say that at one time a Brahman refused to worship Matangi, declaring that he would never do homage to a Madiga, but his entire body broke out in sores and then he capitulated.

In connection with the worship, the Brahmans have a buffalo killed at their own house, which is a most unusual proceeding. The Madigas prepare the buffalo meat, the chief cook tying a cloth over his mouth to prevent any possible contamination from saliva that might be ejected. While the Madigas are preparing the buffalo meat, a washerman brings a goat and prepares its flesh. The Brahmans furnish all pots and other utensils.

When all is ready, the Madigas are first seated, and the Brahman *pujari* serves them with the buffalo meat and other food. After eating, the Madigas goes outside the house and keep up a most frightful din to ward off evil spirits. The Brahman *pujari* now serves the Brahmans to the goat flesh, which they all eat, sitting around the image of Mathamma. They worship the image, and spend the entire night in hearing the stories of Matangi. In the morning they give presents to the Madigas and send them away.

A rather curious story in connection with the worship of Matangi by Brahmans is to the effect that in the village of Oragallu a Brahman, named Patabi Rudrudu, also refused to worship Matangi. All kinds of evils came upon his household. When he enquired the reason he was informed that it was because of his refusal to worship Matangi. He was ordered to arrange for a nine days' festival for her. He himself must be the *bainedu,* or

[11] See page 30.

story-teller. His son must guard the light on the head of the buffalo, and his wife must take the place of the Matangi. All of these offices are performed by Madigas.

The Brahman was further informed that later in the ceremony he himself must be killed, his membranes made into drums, his arms cut off and placed in his mouth, his fat spread over his eyes, and the usual features of the buffalo sacrifice performed. All castes were then to worship Mathamma in her Matangi form. This was all done, and afterwards the Brahman was brought to life, and these various things were done to a buffalo. According to this story the buffalo sacrifice thus originated.

In the greater part of this mixed worship, it appears that the Brahmans are connected with it against their own wishes. Sometimes, however, they appear to profit by the combination, and this is no doubt the reason which has induced them in such instances to interest themselves in ceremonies which they must find revolting.

In the village of Chenduluru, in the Ongole Taluq of Guntur District, is a goddess who is called Maha Lakshmi by the Sudras and Siva Lakshmi by the Brahmans. She is said to have been a Brahman woman who was killed and thrown into a pond because of her evil life. She appeared afterward in the usual way of Dravidian goddesses, and demanded that she be worshiped.

When the goddess is worshiped, the Sudras make an earthen image and the Brahmans one of wood. A booth with two compartments is erected in the center of the village, and the images placed one in each compartment. The Sudras say that at one time they proceeded with the worship of their image without securing the attendance of the Brahman goddess, but the plague was not stayed, and their cattle continued to die in great numbers. After this experience they never again attempted to conduct the worship by themselves. There is a Brahman *pujari* for the wooden image, and he insists that his goddess has not spoken to him until a sufficient amount of money is placed in his hand. The goddess then communicates her wishes and all proceeds. The Sudras must bear all the very considerable expense of the worship.

In another place where the shepherds have a goddess called Yerra Gadipati Ganga, they asked the Brahmans to assist them in the worship. This they consented to do, and raised money from the other castes for the purpose. They took for their fee one-fifth of what they collected. As time went on the offerings grew and the shepherds became dissatisfied with the arrangement. They tried to get the Brahmans to withdraw, but a great quarrel arose in which the Brahmans claimed that the real Ganga was in their homes in the form of a girl ten years old. Soon the shepherds suffered much from thefts, and the Brahmans told them that Ganga was protecting the thieves, and not protecting them.[12] Seeing that their case was hopeless, the shepherds submitted and a Brahman was made *pujari.*

Such are some of the ways in which Brahmanism has been affected. Yet it is remarkable that with all these centuries of association so little mutual influence has resulted. While instances of the making of new local deities, and the stories connected with them, are almost unlimited, these instances of any marked connection between the two religions are rather exceptional. The Brahmans have succeeded in making nominal Hindus of a whole race many times their own in number. They have allowed these people to retain their own religion, and have given the sanctions of Hinduism to their gods and ceremonies; and yet to a great extent they have preserved their own ritual and ceremonies.[13]

[12] The meaning of this explanation was that the Brahmans were sending thieves to harass the shepherds, and that by their superior ability and influence in the village, they were protecting the thieves from punishment. I am told by those who know the customs of the people well that this is not at all uncommon.

[13] The influence of Hinduism on Mohammedanism is an interesting subject for study in this connection. That there has been such influence is very evident. Moreover it is the Dravidian form of worship which has appealed to the Mohammedans rather than the Brahmanic form. One reason for this is that many of the Mohammedans of South India are converts from Dravidian beliefs. Another reason is the exclusiveness of Brahmanism, which would debar all Mohammedans as outcastes from its ceremonies. *The Census of India.* 1911, Vol. XII, pt. 1, para. 40, says, "Whether from design or from the insensible influence of environment,

## CHAPTER XII

### Fundamental Conceptions in Dravidian Worship

No adequate knowledge of the origin of Dravidian worship will perhaps ever be secured. There are no writings or other records which give assistance. No monuments of any great importance have been left. No buried cities have ever been discovered. We can only say that at the time of the Aryan invasion the Dravidians were worshipers of deities which the Aryans called "mad gods." The persistence of the peculiar forms of their worship to the present time, after centuries of close contact with Hinduism, and while later surrounded with a fair degree of modern enlightenment, indicates that the "mad gods" worshiped when the Aryans came to India were very much the same as the deities described in the preceding pages.

We are interested, however, more in the meaning of these ceremonies than in the date of their origin. What were the motives and beliefs which originated the ritual? What were the ideas behind this worship, and whence did these ideas come? In Hinduism we are not at all left in the dark as to this question. From the Vedas we learn that the great powers of nature so impressed the Aryans that such powers were deified. From this august nature-worship has grown the present system. In the Dravidian religion, however, we are not so fortunate as to have left us any ancient hymns or any systems of philosophy. No great interpreters of their religion have arisen. We are confined to one

there can be no doubt that certain compromises now exist in Madras between Hinduism and Mohammedanism. Propitiation of disease godlings, worship of patron saints and local deities, veneration of relics, practisings of the black art, divinations of the future, Hindu ceremonies at birth and death; all practises satirized by the poet Hali, abound throughout the Presidency, and render the stern simplicity of Islam more attractive for its rural followers." William Crooke (*Things Indian*, p. 337 sq.) gives instances of the same tendencies. See also *Gazetteer of Madura District*, I, p. 80.

source, the induction which may be made from the legends and ceremonies as we now have them.

DID THE SACRIFICES ORIGINATE IN TOTEMISM? Bishop Whitehead[1] presents the theory of a totemistic origin of the present sacrifices as one which will best explain the peculiar customs. He says that this theory is only a hypothesis, but he feels that it is the best hypothesis yet suggested.

The argument for a totemistic origin is as follows. In the primitive stage men wished to be brothers not only to the other tribes, but also to the beasts, and often this was brought about by an exchange of blood. In the Dravidian sacrifices, especially the buffalo sacrifice, the victim is often worshiped and garlanded. There is a feast in the presence of the deity. The blood of the sacrifice is often applied to the worshipers, their houses, and cattle, and is sometimes mixed with rice and scattered on the streets or boundaries. The entrails of the buffalo are placed about the neck of a Madiga, and with the vitals in his mouth, he goes to the boundaries. All this, it is thought, may be best explained, not by any gift theory of sacrifice, but as the remnants of an original desire to come into close blood relations with the sacrifice itself.

In the consideration of this question of totemism, an investigation of the meaning of the buffalo sacrifice will be useful. The buffalo sacrifice in one of the most constant features of Dravidian worship. Numbers of buffalos, sheep, goats, and chickens may be offered, but there is but one offering to which the name of *devara potu,* or "The Buffalo Sacrifice," is properly given. That is the only buffalo which, in addition to being beheaded, has its legs cut off and placed in its mouth and the fat from its abdomen spread over its eyes.

We are no doubt a long distance from having found any explanation of the incident or custom from which this peculiar and persistent rite has arisen. The legends concerning the buffalo sacrifice will, however, give us some assistance in learning what its fundamental ideas may have been. Some of these may now be given.

[1] *Madras Government Museum, Bulletin,* V, no. 3, pp. 179 sq.

In former times there was a Brahman living in an *agraharamu*,[2] who had one daughter. One day a young man came, saying that he was a Brahman and wished to study. The Brahman received him and taught him for years. The young man was, however, a Pariah, a Mala according to the most common version of the story. In the course of time the Brahman's daughter became infatuated with him and married him.

Some years later the young man's mother came to visit them. Her son warned her not to reveal his low origin. He had her shaved and dressed as a Brahman widow, and told his wife that she was deaf and dumb. All went well until one day the daughter-in-law prepared a dish in which flour and water are formed into long strings somewhat like macaroni. When the old woman saw it she forgot to be silent and asked if it was the entrails of animals, a dish with which she would not be unfamiliar. Another version runs that on a feast day she asked if certain sweetmeats were fish tongues.

The suspicions of the daughter-in-law were aroused, and her husband could not deny her accusations. She went to her father and asked what should be done to purify a pot if a dog had licked it. Her father replied that the only way was to cast the pot into the fire. She understood his meaning, and soon after having sent her mother-in-law and children away for a time, she shut herself in the house and burned the house and herself.

The spirit of the dead woman now appeared in the center of the village, and after rebuking the people for allowing her to marry a Pariah, she gave directions for her worship. She further told them that her husband should be beheaded, one of his hands placed in his mouth, the fat from his abdomen placed over his eyes, and a light placed on his head before her.

The villagers accordingly seized her husband, and after leading him about the village, beheaded him according to her directions. Her children were then brought before her. According to one story she had no mercy on them because they were the children of a Pariah, and ordered them to be slain. They are now repre-

[2] An *agraharamu* is a village set apart exclusively for Brahmans.

sented by the sheep and goats which are offered to the goddess, as the husband is represented by the buffalo. Another and more pleasing legend is to the effect that she said the children were hers and should not be injured, but that they should become *asadis*. The present Madiga horn-blowers accept this tale and claim to be the descendants of these children.

This legend is attached to almost every one of the local deities.[3] It certainly gives no hint of a totemistic origin for the buffalo sacrifice.[4] Here is another story, not nearly so common, however.

There was once a village king who did not worship Poleramma. She reproved him for his neglect, and he made an agreement with her that the matter should be decided by a fight between her and the king's buffalo. If she should be successful in the fight he promised to worship her, but if she were defeated she must worship the king.

Poleramma now took human form, and the fight began. The buffalo was getting the best of the fight, and so Poleramma fled to an ant-hill and took refuge there. The buffalo followed with its lumbering gait, but by the time he arrived at the ant-hill Poleramma could not be seen. He put his front feet on the ant-hill and peered into it, but could see no one. He now asked some sheep and lambs which were grazing near by, to tell him what had become of Poleramma. They informed him that she had gone into the hill.

The buffalo waited with his feet on the ant-hill, but Poleramma did not come out. Finally the time set for the battle was up, and Poleramma appeared and claimed victory for what would seem at least to be a drawn battle. She maintained that the fight was to

[3] *Kurnool District Manual*, sec. 6, pp. 100–103 gives this story with some variations as applying to Sunkulamma. Oppert, *Original Inhabitants of India*, p. 485, attaches the story to Ankamma. *Madras Government Museum, Bulletin*, V, no. 3, pp. 119, 120, says the story is told of Ur-Amma as well as other gods.

[4] This story is given in the *Mural Mahathmam*. It is much as related here up to the death of the woman, who was then honored by becoming Vishnu's flute. The account of her appearing as a ghost and demanding the buffalo sacrifice is entirely Dravidian.

be to the death, and the buffalo had not killed her within the allotted time.

Poleramma now reiterated her demand for worship, and gave the following directions. "When you worship me you must certainly kill a buffalo in remembrance of this fight. The lambs and sheep informed the buffalo that I went into the hill, so they also must be sacrificed. If I see the eyes of the dead buffalo I shall be afraid, so you must open its abdomen and with its fat cover its eyes. If I see the mouth I shall be afraid, so you must put the legs in the mouth. You must also put a light on its head in honor of me." The king obeyed, and this has been the order of worship ever since.

This story does not seem to be very consistent. The fat spread over the eyes and the legs crossed in the mouth of the dead buffalo surely do not decrease the unpleasantness of the sight. Again, however, there seems to be no totemistic connection. The sacrificed buffalo is a conquered enemy.

When we turn to the Hindu and Puranic legends we find the buffalo mentioned occasionally, and it is a marked coincidence that in every case the buffalo is an enemy and is destroyed. In the *Ramayana*[5] the fierce buffalo, Dundubhi, is a demon incarnate. He tore up with his horns the cavern of Bali, son of Indra, and king of the monkeys. Bali seized him by the horns, and after a terrible struggle dashed him to pieces.

Another legend, as told in the Markandaya Purana,[6] relates that Diti, the mother of the Asuras, lost all of her sons in a fight with the gods. Another son was born to her, and he took the form of a buffalo in order to annihilate the gods. He was called Mahisasura. The story goes on to tell of the terrible fight between Durga and this buffalo. Durga at last conquered him, and cutting off his head, drank his blood.

A similar legend is connected with the defeat of the Rakshasas by Renuka.[7] When she returned victorious to her father, she

[5] Griffith, *The Ramayan of Valmiki*. Bk. IV, Canto XI, pp. 335 sq.

[6] *Durga Sapta Shati*, in the *Markandaya Purana*, Bangalore, 1893, pp. 22 sq. (Sanskrit).

[7] See page 90.

brought the head of the chief Rakshasa in her hand. The Dravidian version adds that his hands had been cut off and placed in his mouth, while his eyes were covered with fat from his own abdomen.

Oppert[8] gives the following story of Peddamma. In the beginning there was only light. By meditation light produced a woman, who was placed in a beautiful garden. Desiring a husband she picked a jassamine flower, placed it on a lotus, and becoming a bird, hovered over it. Soon three eggs appeared. In seventy-two days one egg opened and became the earth and sky. The yolk of this egg became the sun and moon. From a black speck in the egg Brahma, Siva, and Vishnu were born. Soon the second egg opened and the Rakshasas came from it. The third egg addled and brought forth diseases.

The legend then tells of the desire of this woman for the three gods, in consequence of which she suffered the curse of becoming prematurely old. Her passion was now gone, and she determined to destroy the Rakshasas. She slew many, but a new one sprang up for every drop of blood which fell to the ground. She spread out her own tongue for a distance of one hundred and twenty miles to catch the blood.[9] Now she was successful and had the Rakshasas all but conquered, when another drop fell and produced Dundubhi, the buffalo demon.

Dundubhi now fought with the gods, seriously defeating them. He blew away the chariots of Brahma, Vishnu, and Siva with his breath. Peddamma, the original woman, now attacked him. She had seven arms,[10] and after various forms of contest, she created an ant-hill into which she disappeared as an ichneumon. She now led up from the under world ninety million Siddhalu, or demigods, who by their chanting as they came up, scared the buffalo demon to death.

The Siddhalu now cut off the head of the buffalo, put its leg in its mouth, spread the fat over the eyes, and from the buffalo's own fat made oil with which to feed the light placed on its head.

[8] *Original Inhabitants of India*, pp. 472 sq.

[9] Compare the story of Potu Razu, page 90.

[10] This probably identifies Pedamma with Durgamma who had ten arms.

The head was placed before Peddamma as an offering, and the Siddhalu cut up the body of the buffalo and made a feast.[11]

From such legends as these we may not hope to establish any historical facts about the origin and meaning of the buffalo sacrifice. We may get, however, what is almost as valuable. We may get a psychological view of the motives behind it. The object of the buffalo sacrifice as shown in these legends cannot be that of any desire for fellowship with the sacrifice. In every case, both in the modern and the Puranic legends, the sacrifice represents the dire punishment and disgrace of a conquered enemy. It is remarkable that the god should be honored by the dishonoring of the sacrifice. What could be more of a dishonor than to have one's own hands cut off and crossed in the mouth of his decapitated head, while his own fat, probably representing his strength, is spread over his eyes, and his own body must furnish the oil for the light to be placed before the victor? This is the supreme humiliation of a feared, despised, and defeated enemy.

The disposition of the carcass also shows this dishonor. The sheep and the chickens are eaten by the givers, often with much merry-making. But the body of the buffalo is dragged away at night by the Pariahs for an unclean feast, and at times it is not disposed of by them until after decomposition sets in.

In all the legends of the buffalo sacrifice, the buffalo represents a fallen enemy. May this not be the historical origin of the strange rites? As Renuka returned from her victories carrying her enemy's head in her hand, with the fat over his eyes and his now useless hands in his mouth, unable to see, speak, or fight, so in

[11] Bishop Whitehead (*Madras Government Museum, Bulletin*, V, no. 3, p. 132) tells of a custom in which the buffalo is cut up and a part of the flesh is cooked. This, with some cooked *cholam*, is given to five little Mala boys called Siddhalu, who eat it. While eating they are covered with a large cloth so as to be concealed from view. He suggests that the reason for the covering may be to prevent interference from spirits or the evil eye. It seems quite probable that, while no doubt this may be the explanation now in the minds of the people, the origin of the custom is connected with the above story, and the covered place represents the under-world where the Siddhalu dwell unseen, and from which they came to the help of Peddamma.

the struggles of the early days of the Dravidians this may have been their method of showing complete victory over the himiliated enemy.

The gods of the Dravidians are almost universally human beings returned to earth. As in their lifetime the triumph over an enemy was the greatest of honors, so now as gods a sacrifice representing such honors would be thought to be of all things most pleasing. After the head of the buffalo has been cut off the eyes are often watched until they blink in death. A great shout is then raised, as the blinking of the eyes is said to be a sign that the offering is now acceptable to the goddess. May not the blinking of the eyes be the last act of submission by the conquered enemy?

The peculiar features of the sacrifice which are explained by totemism may perhaps be as well explained by this theory of a conquered enemy. The buffalo has a garland placed about its neck, *botlu* are placed on its head, and as it is led about the village, people bow before it placing their hands in the attitude of worship. This apparent worship is often omitted, and does not appear to be an essential. This procession about the village in which the buffalo is led with a garland about its neck, may very possibly be the remnant of a triumphal procession in which the enemy was exhibited before the disgraceful death. The only explanation which the people appear to know is that this makes the offering acceptable to the goddess. This explanation agrees better with the theory of a conquered enemy than with the theory of totemism. The apparent worship of the animal, when it occurs, may very possibly be a later addition, arising from the Hindu idea of pantheism and the sacredness of all life.

The feast in the presence of the deity, according to the totemistic hypothesis, is for the purpose of communion with the deity. This no doubt is the object of the feast, or perhaps to indicate that peace has been established. It is communion or peace with the deity, not with the sacrificed animal, however, which is desired. This feast does not often take place in direct connection with the buffalo sacrifice, and probably needs no further explanation than that in all lands a common meal is the seal of friendship, and as the Dravidian gods are exceedingly anthropomorphic, naturally such a feast would help to avert any evils which they were planning. It is quite probable that the buffalo sacrifice and the feast were entirely distinct features originally, and no common explanation need be sought.

The use of the blood, worshipers smearing it upon themselves at times, spattering it on their houses, or scattering bloody rice on the boundaries, appears to be explained by totemism in that the worshipers seek a blood relationship with the deity. It should again be noticed that any connection established by such uses of the blood is with the goddess, and not with the animal sacrificed.

The Dravidian goddesses are always bloodthirsty. It has been seen that in some cases blood is poured into the mouth of the image, or the *pujari,* as representing the goddess, drinks the blood.[12] The smearing of blood upon the person, or sprinkling it upon houses and cattle, is probably an effort to get the full benefit of the sacrifice. The person or thing thus anointed would receive special favor from the deity.

The totemistic theory explains the hideous custom of wrapping the entrails about the neck and taking the vitals in the mouth as an effort to get into closer touch with the life of the totem animal. This explanation appears to be based on a misconception of the intention in carrying the bloody rice to the boundaries. This bloody rice is a real offering to the bloodthirsty devils and Saktis which may have been aroused by the ceremonies going on inside the village. It is a dangerous matter to deal with these devils, and the man who is brave enough to undertake it must do everything to protect himself. He makes himself as hideous as possible, hoping that the devils will think that he is a stronger devil than they. Even then he is in terrible danger, and sacrifices are offered whenever he cries out that he sees devils. At last he swoons and is revived with great difficulty because of the dangers to which he has been exposed.[13]

[12] See Ankamma, page 25 and Kati Ankamma, 41.

[13] See page 40. Oppert (*Original Inhabitants of India,* p. 462) says that the *pujari* throws a handful of bloody rice into every back yard at midnight to keep off the devils.

It may further be noticed that in South India the buffalo is not considered an honorable animal, though a very useful one. It is stupid, ungainly, ugly in appearance, sometimes vicious, and is noted for having the least sense of all domesticated animals. To call one a buffalo is to offer the greatest insult. Before it was domesticated it may have been a terror to the people, for the buffalo was the vehicle of Yama, the god of death.[14] This is not the kind of an animal to become a totem. The monkey, which is never killed or used as a sacrifice, but which is often worshiped, is a much more probable totem. It appears, therefore, from the foregoing reasons, that the buffalo sacrifice at least did not originate in totemism.

FETISHISM IN THE DRAVIDIAN RELIGION. Much of the Dravidian worship is often classed as fetishism. The fetish worshiper of Africa selects any object which strikes his fancy, especially an unusual object, and makes it his fetish. When it appears to be no longer helping him, he throws it away, thinking that its spirit has left it. The objects of worship of the Dravidians bear some resemblance to the fetishes of Africa. Often the idol is a shapeless stone.[15] Like the African, the Dravidian deserts his god, leaving it on the boundary of the village, or the rubbish heap.[16]

[14] *Ibid.*, p. 461. Crooke, *The Popular Religion and Folklore of Northern India*, II, p. 169, tells the same, and also says that at times the buffalo is made a scapegoat to carry away disease.

[15] In Chagollu, Nellore District, I found Vinaiyakudu, the god of the grain, represented by some dried cow-dung tied together with a saffron colored string. Men were taking rice from the bin, and this image, which had been kept in the bin, was carefully placed at one side to be used again. I was informed that the image would double the crop. This seems much like fetishism, but while the people were Dravidians, it appears that Vinaiyakudu is more Hindu than Dravidian. I can find no local stories of his birth, but he is said to be the son of Iswara. He has no bloody offerings.

[16] Sir Alfred Lyall, *Asiatic Studies*, First Series, p. 10, gives an exhaustive classification of the worship in Berar, Central India. It is as follows.

1. The worship of mere stocks and stones, and of local configurations, which are unusual or grotesque in size, shape, or position.
2. The worship of things inanimate which are gifted with mysterious motion.
3. The worship of animals which are feared.

There is, however, a fundamental difference in the conception of the Dravidian and the African. The fetish of the African possesses a spirit of its own, and this spirit is worshiped because it has been found useful to the one possessing the fetish. When this spirit inhabiting the fetish is found to be no longer useful, the fetish is discarded.

The idol of the Dravidian also possesses a spirit, but it is simply the abiding place of the spirit, usually a ghost. The spirit is in no sense the spirit of the object or idol. Moreover, the Dravidian does not worship his idol for good luck or prosperity. He worships in order to avert calamity; to pacify the deity so that his prosperity will not be interfered with.[17] The final object of his worship is to secure prosperity, but his thought is not that the god will bring him prosperity, but must rather be prevented from interfering with his welfare. When the Dravidian throws away

4. The worship of visible things, animate or inanimate, which are directly or indirectly useful and profitable, or which possess any incomprehensible function or property.

5. The worship of a *deo*, or spirit, a thing without form, and void—the vague impersonation of the uncanny sensation which comes over one at certain places.

6. The worship of dead relatives, and other deceased persons known in their lifetime to the worshiper.

7. The worship of persons who had a great reputation during life, or who died in some strange and notorious way—at shrines.

8. The worship in temples of the persons belonging to the foregoing class, as demigods, or subordinate deities.

9. The worship of manifold local incarnations of the elder deities and their symbols.

10. The worship of departmental deities.

11. The worship of the supreme gods of Hinduism.

He speaks of 1–4 in the above classification as fetishism. The worship which he describes under these headings, however, is Hindu rather than Dravidian. Under 6–8 he describes what comes largely under the head of Dravidian ceremonies, and he does not mention these as connected with fetishism. The Hindu conception of pantheism seems to lend itself to fetishism more readily than does the Dravidian spirit worship.

[17] In the festival of Gowry, people worship their implements. This is, however, a Hindu feast, not Dravidian. This worship of implements is very close to fetishism. See *Manual of Administration of the Madras Presidency*, I, p. 75.

the idol it is not because he is dissatisfied with it, but because it has served its purpose, and the deity is no longer in it. When he leaves it on the boundaries, it is always with great honor, and in the hope that the spirit will not come again into the village.

It is undoubtedly true that the Dravidians have some measure of fetishism in their religious ideas.[18] There is no religion but what has at some stage possessed considerable fetishism, and strangely enough, those which are usually considered the more advanced religious systems have a large amount of fetishism in their corrupted forms, if not in their original conceptions. It is indeed striking, however, that the fundamental ideas of the Dravidians, as shown in their worship and the stories of their gods, contain so little fetishism, which is commonly thought to be an invariable feature in primitive religion.[19]

DRAVIDIAN ANIMISM. The term animism has been chosen to represent the peculiar religious ideas of the Dravidians.[20] It was

18 Cf. the story of Kulagollamma, page 78. I once visited a village where there were no Brahmans, and noticed that Ramaswami's temple was empty. In answer to my enquiries the people laughed and said, "Oh, Ramaswami did not send us any rain last year, so we got tired of him and threw him into the cactus." Ramaswami is a Hindu god who has been largely adopted by the Dravidians. He has never taken a very strong hold on the people. There is no danger that the Dravidian village deity will ever be thus thrown away.

19 On the entire subject see Monier-Williams, *Brahmanism and Hinduism*, p. 340; F. Max Müller, *Lectures on the Origin of Religion*, London, 1891, Lect. II, pp. 54 sq.

20 *Madras Census Report*, 1891, Ch. III, p. 88. "The term 'animistic' was suggested by the Census Commission to denote the religion of those forest and hill tribes whose religious beliefs show no trace of orthodox Hinduism. In 1881 this religion was called 'aboriginal,' an expression to which exception has been taken on the ground that there are many aboriginal tribes who are recognized to be Hindus by religion. But the term 'animistic' is equally open to objection in that there are many people invariably recognized as Hindus whose real religion is almost pure animism. I take 'animism' to mean a belief in the existence of souls, with the addition that after death the soul remains in the neighborhood where it dwelt when incarnate, and is active for good and evil. The souls of dead ancestors must be worshiped and provided with sacrifices of animals and offerings of other kinds of food, or otherwise evil will befall the members of the family to whom the soul belonged."

at first applied to the tribes which have not at all come within Hinduism, but the Dravidians who have come have brought with them the same practices, and therefore their religion must be termed animistic.[21] Animism is not altogether a satisfactory term in this connection, for as usually understood it does not accurately describe the Dravidian conception.[22] Tylor defines it as the belief that inanimate objects and the phenomena of nature are endowed with personal life or a living soul. This approaches more to fetishism. In fact, it is difficult to draw any hard and fast lines between animism and fetishism.[23] The *Travencore State Manual*[24] says that animism differs from fetishism in that it is the spirit which is feared, while in fetishism it is the object which has supernatural powers.[25]

The "people invariably recognized as Hindus" mentioned in this quotation are the Dravidians, almost exclusively. We have seen, however, that it is not especially the dead ancestors who are worshiped. Such an origin for a Dravidian god would be a marked exception.

[21] *Census of 1911*, Vol. XII, Pt. 1, paras. 86–103, gives an account of the Khonds, a hill tribe which has not come into Hinduism. Their home is in the Nalamalli Hills. In this tribe may be found all the fundamental ideas of the worship of local deities such as have been described in the preceding pages. There is no belief in Karma or Transmigration, which comes only from philosophical Hinduism. There is a god who guards the village from the outside, and a helper who receives a fee of fowls and eggs. These seem like Poleramma and Potu Razu. There are numerous gods which brings various diseases, and connected with their various kinds of property. Paragraph 96 says, "It may be that the Khonds' hilly country, with its feverish climate, has prevented the intersection of its orbit with that of so-called Hinduism. Did opportunity offer, the Khond would probably enter the Hindu fold, bringing with him his gods, as easily as many another Dravidian demon worshiper has done, and receive in time a tincture of deeper and more spiritual religious ideas, with a greater fixity and seemliness of his social relations."

[22] *The Travencore State Manual*, II, p. 39, says, "Animism is an exceedingly crude form of religion in which magic or the propitiation of the unknown predominates. . . . According to Prof. Tiele of Leyden, animism is the belief in the existence of souls or spirits of which only the powerful acquire the rank of divine beings and become objects of worship. They are free, or may take up their abode in any object, living or inanimate."

[23] Monier-Williams, *Brahmanism and Hinduism*, p. 340.

[24] *Travencore State Manual*, II, p. 39.

[25] *Census of India*, 1901, I, p. 358, gives an interesting account of clerks

As the Census Commission of India has adopted the term, animism, for the Dravidian religion, we need not hesitate to use that designation, perhaps modifying it to Dravidian animism. It will be well, however, to examine somewhat more closely the fundamental conceptions of this Dravidian animism.

DRAVIDIAN DEMONOLATRY. In Dravidian animism there are two outstanding characteristics: the spirits are always from outside the object of worship, not being the spirits of the objects themselves; and these spirits quite generally have a human origin. The term, demonolatry, comes more close to describing the underlying Dravidian ideas than does any other one expression. By demonolatry we must not understand only what is ordinarily called "devil worship." The *dayyamu* is a spirit, not necessarily an evil spirit.[26] In practice, of course, it is the evil spirits which secure the most attention, for it is fear of them which calls forth the ceremonies of propitiation. It is, therefore, by a consideration of the Dravidian fear of evil-minded spirits that we shall find the key to practically all of the ideas and customs connected with their worship.[27]

The customs connected with the Matangi[28] are striking, and various explanations have been offered. We may see if the belief in demonolatry will explain these.

What can be the meaning of the strange procedure of the Matangi as she rushes about, touching the people with her wand, backing into them, and, worst of all, spitting upon them? She is a Madiga, whose very touch is pollution to a Brahman. Moreover there is nothing more polluting than saliva. A Brahman will

worshiping a foreign ink bottle, pens, and stationary. This is said to be a form of animism. It should be remembered that clerks in India are almost exclusively Brahmans. It is not probable that any Dravidians were among those of whom this is told.

For an excellent discussion of animistic religions in India, see Ch. VIII of this Census Report.

[26] See note 2, page 51.

[27] *Manual of Administration of Madras Presidency*, I, p. 76: "The real worship of the population consists in doing homage either to demons to avert their displeasure, or to deities who rule such demons, to induce their interposition. The former worship is more constant than the latter."

[28] See page 30.

be thrown into a panic if a leaf plate which has been used chances to fall in front of his door. The people eat with their fingers, and it is considered that the saliva has come into contact with the plate. This is what makes it so objectionable, as saliva is most polluting.[29] Why then this willingness and even eagerness to be spat upon by a Madiga woman?

It is commonly said that this contact with the Matangi is for purification, but at the same time the Brahmans say that Matangi is a great devil. These two statements do not agree. The most probable explanation is that the Brahmans have come to possess the same fear of this devil that the Dravidians have of all their demon goddesses, and the willingness to be spat upon is in order to escape from some evil which might come from the Matangi.

By the Matangi spitting upon the people, she renders them immune in two ways. First, as the Matangi is a terrible devil herself, it is well to have her favor, even though it must be secured in so unpleasant a manner. A second result is that after she has spat upon the people no other demon would think them worth spending time upon. Anyone who would consent to be spat upon by a Madiga woman surely would be poor prey for other demons. The haste of the Brahman household to be rid of her, their willingness to give her plenty of presents, and their meek submission while she sings wildly and exultingly of their humiliation, all agree with this idea of their fear of her, and not at all with the statement that her spittle is purifying.

The fear of the evil eye among the Dravidians is most easily explained by this fear of evil spirits.[30] A common explanation of

[29] One evening in a village I saw a great commotion in front of a Brahman's house. An old Brahman, the head of the house, was jabbing at something most excitedly and savagely with a long stick, while all the family were gathered around in great excitement. I thought that he must be killing a cobra, and wondered at that, as Brahmans will not kill anything, most of all the sacred snake. Upon coming nearer I found that all this consternation was caused by a used leaf plate which the wind or a dog had left before his gate. He was trying to remove it with the stick, and finally succeeded in piercing it, when he carried it at the end of the pole to a distant rubbish heap.

[30] For excellent descriptions of the various customs connected with the evil eye in India see Dubois, *Hindu Manners, Customs and Ceremonies,*

the evil eye is that a person may have some evil influence which is communicated by a look. This is called *drishti-dosha.* Undoubtedly there is some such fear of the look of a human being, especially if he be a stranger. This conception of the evil eye appears to be more Brahmanic than Dravidian. The most of the Dravidian customs connected with the evil eye can with difficulty be explained by the evil resulting from a look, while the explanation becomes very simple if the fear of evil spirits is postulated as the basis.

The Dravidian idea of the evil eye is that there are innumerable evil spirits waiting at all times to do harm. These spirits appear to be very much dependent on human suggestion and initiative. If special attention is directed to any object or person, and especially if something complimentary is said about it, some listening spirit will take notice, and thinking the object is desirable for itself, or out of jealousy and evil mindedness, will bring about some evil.

One can scarcely do a more untactful thing in India than to praise a man's crops or cattle or child.[31] The proper thing to do is not to appear to pay too much attention to that which interests you, or if it is necessary to mention it, mention some defect. This is one of the reasons for wearing ornaments, and it is always in order to praise or notice the ornaments on a child, as this will keep attention away from the child itself. The gracious friend always addresses one with words of commiseration because he is looking so poorly. The European is often disappointed because his Indian friends see nothing but faults in his new horse or house, when he expects them to praise it.

With the idea of making the spirits think an article is worthless some flaw is left in everything. No house is ever completed. The weaver leaves a flaw in his cloth. The brickmaker daubs his kiln with unsightly spots of lime. The placing of obscene figures and carvings on idol cars and temples is often explained in the

Oxford, 1899, p. 152; Thurston, *Omens and Superstitions of Southern India,* London, 1912, pp. 109–120; Crooke, *Things Indian,* New York, 1906, pp. 192–195; Monier-Williams, *Brahmanism and Hinduism,* pp. 253, 254.

[31] When I first came to India I at one time thought to please a mother by complimenting her attractive child, but the mother seized the child and ran away with it in terrible fright.

same way. Crooke says this is the reason for blackening the under lids of the eyes, which is very common among well-to-do women.[32]

The names of children often seem most unsuitable. Such names as Pichchiah meaning crazy man, Dibbiah meaning rubbish heap, Roshiah meaning an ill-tempered man, Musaliah meaning old, decrepit man, are common. The reason for giving these names is that there have been deaths among the former children, and it is hoped that by thus giving the new child a bad name the evil spirits will think that it has no desirable qualities, and so not molest it.[33] At times a boy will be dressed in girl's clothing in order to deceive the spirits.

Still other devices are adopted to deceive the spirits regarding children. When two children have died it is a common custom to roll the third in the dust to make it very undesirable in appearance. It is then named Kuppiah, which means rubbish. At the time of marriage such a child will be disfigured or disguised, still further to prevent the demons from doing any injury.[34] At other times a new-born child will be given to a Yanadi woman. She is told that the child is useless, and she takes it away. Soon after she appears at the door with the child, saying that it is hers and asking the parents to take it and rear it as she is poor and cannot do so. They indignantly refuse, and then she places the child on the rubbish heap. After a time some member of the family will go and bring the child in, saying that it is too bad to let it perish, even though it is only a poor Yanadi. They name the child Yanadi, and raise it in the usual way. All this is supposed to throw the eager spirits off the track, and so save the child.[35]

A pot smeared with whitewash is often placed in a field of grain to protect from the evil eye. Such pots are also placed on the housetops. In other cases strange images are placed in the

[32] Crooke, *Popular Religion and Folklore of Northern India*, II, pp. 3 ff.

[33] The writer was one time working with a Brahman pundit named Pichchiah. In response to my question about his name he replied that three children before him had died, and so his parents named him Pichchiah with the result that he had survived.

[34] *Gazetteer of Tanjore*, I, p. 67.

[35] In north India when one child has died the next is placed in a sieve and dragged around the house to baffle the evil eye.

PLATE VIII

AN IMAGE TO AVERT THE EVIL EYE

This image is for the protection of the ripening grain. It appears to be a scare-crow, but it is not for the purpose of scaring birds. It is expected that this image will attract attention and so divert evil from the grain.

fields. Very often these images are exceedingly obscene.[36] The usual explanation is that the object first seen will utilize all the evil in the look, and these objects will first attract attention. There is some reason to believe that before pots were used for these purposes human skulls were placed in the fields. If this was the origin it certainly must have been with the purpose of making the demons think the spot was an undesirable place, perhaps a cemetery. The strange images which look like scarecrows probably originated in the same idea. Their hideous appearance is thought to deceive the spirits. The obscene images are more difficult to explain. Taking account of the state of Dravidian morality, and that the spirits were once human beings, it is probable that the original idea was that the spirts would have so much interest in these figures that they would not proceed further.

Akin to the reason for the fear of the evil eye are other peculiar customs which have been described in the preceding pages. In the worship of Bangaramma,[37] and also occasionally in that of other gods, the Madigas revile the higher castes. If they hesitate to do this they are compelled to begin their vituperation. The reason is the same as the desire to be spat upon by the Matangi, and to have no complimentary word spoken of one. That reason is that listening evil spirits may hear the vile epithets spoken by despised outcastes, and so drop all interest in those who are reviled.

The ordinary worship of Dravidian local deities is easily understood on the hypothesis of demonolatry. The usual object of worship is to stop some epidemic or other trouble which has appeared in the village. The deity concerned is angry and must be propitiated. In the case of the village deity the cause of the anger may be that she is expecting offerings. In the case of a visiting goddess like Kanaka Durgamma, the offering is to induce her to leave peaceably. In any case the goddess is an evil-bringing demoness, and the worship is to propitiate her.[38]

[36] See Crooke, *Things Indian*, pp. 114 sq. At one time I was able to persuade the villagers of the evil effects of such an image and they removed it.

[37] See page 27.

[38] I have tried to find in the worship at least some measure of gratitude

Such ceremonies as those performed in times of epidemics are easily understood in the light of this explanation. A piece of cactus is often placed on the wall or hung over the door. This is done so that the demon bringing the disease will think the place deserted and pass it by. In some places the people suspend small pots of toddy from the eaves of the house. The intention appears to be that the spirits will drink this, and being satisfied will pass on. Another suggested explanation is that the spirits will certainly think a place deserted where toddy is left untouched!

In this way it would be possible to go through all the ceremonies described in the preceding chapters and in every case, from the worship of the most benign Perantalu to the propitiation of the most hideous devil, the simple explanation would be found to be the belief in and worship of spirits and spirits only.

THE MEANING OF THE IDOLS. It seems strange that a spirit should be represented by a stone or other image, often shapeless and uncarved, and quite unconnected with the history of the spirit in any way. The popular conception of Dravidian worship on the part of the majority of Europeans, is that it belongs under Lyall's first heading, the worship of "stocks and stones."[39] We see the throngs of people bowing before an image and making offerings to it and naturally think that this constitutes all their worship.

Contrary to the popular idea, however, the worship of "stocks and stones" is far more the tendency of Hindus than of Dravidians. The Hindu is a pantheist. To him deity appears in all objects, animate and inanimate. He does not hesitate to support

for the protection which the goddess has given, but so far without success. The worship appears to be totally for propitiation in order to escape the present or impending evil. J. A. Curtis of Donokonda writes, "I do not remember a single phrase or experience that would justify assigning 'a certain degree of thankfulness' to any of these religious acts." *The Journal of the Anthropological Society of Bombay*, VII, p. 502, says, "The sole object of the worship of these village deities is to propitiate them and avert their wrath. There is no idea of praise or thanksgiving, no expression of gratitude and love, no desire for any moral or spiritual blessings. The one object is to get rid of the cholera or small pox or cattle disease or drought, or to avert some of the minor evils of life."

[39] See note 16, page 131.

idolatry on the ground that deity is present in everything, and that it is therefore justifiable to worship any object which is convenient or desirable.

The Dravidian idea is not the same. In the foregoing chapters we have seen no instance of the worship of any object as an object, or because of the spirit of the object. In every case the worship is addressed to an outside spirit which has taken up its residence, temporary or otherwise, in the object. The Dravidian makes a god for the day and throws it away, or leaves it on the boundaries. After the one day it is nothing, and the cattle may trample it under foot. This by no means indicates that the deity is discarded. It cannot be that the image is the object of worship. We see a company of people placing *botlu* on a tree and making offerings before it, and it appears that they are worshiping the tree. It is not the tree, however, but the spirits in the tree, that they are worshiping.[40] Tree worship as such is Hindu, not Dravidian.

It is very evident, therefore, that the Dravidian is not a worshiper of "stocks and stones." He is a worshiper of spirits. The question then arises as to the connection between the spirit worshiped, and the image, often shapeless and uncarved, and quite unconnected with the history of the spirit. The totemistic theory explains the image as being at first placed to mark the spot where the totem animal was killed to insure the presence of its spirit. The place became taboo, and needed some such symbol to prevent it from any violation. In course of time the original significance was lost, and the stone itself was considered to be the deity.

My investigations lead me to believe that, while the stone was not the original deity, and while it was erected to mark a particular spot, that spot was not the scene of the sacrifice of a totem

[40] See page 35. *Manual of Administration of Madras Presidency,* I, p. 71, says trees are worshiped because they are supposed to be the abode of gods. In South India it is thought that the superior gods live in groves, and demons in single trees. This is probably an inaccurate distinction between the gods of Hinduism and of the Dravidians. The *Gazetteer of South Arcot,* I, p. 102, says that *puja* is made to the *margosa* tree, apparently, but really to Maramma who dwells in the tree. The Valaiyans in their backyards have a tree, *Odina wodier,* in which devils are thought to live. These devils are propitiated once a year. *Gazetteer of Tanjore,* I, p. 69.

animal, but rather the place where a spirit first appeared. The difficulty with the totemistic theory is that to this day the stone is not worshiped, and so no transference of worship from the totem animal to the stone can be assumed. It is the spirit which has come to dwell in the stone that is worshiped, and that spirit has no connection with a totem.

The legends which have been given of the formation of new deities all indicate that the stone marks the place where the spirit appeared, or the place chosen for its residence. Commonly a shrine or temple is erected over the stone, but this is by no means essential. Often the stone is changed, or the same stone has an image graven on it long after it was first erected.[41]

After the place was marked by a stone, the dwelling place of the spirit appears to have been gradually narrowed to the stone itself. The idea has then developed that the spirit may be induced to take up its residence, temporary or otherwise, in the prepared image, and in this form receive the homage of the people. It can not be denied that, by long association with the image it inhabits, the spirit has become identified with the image in the minds of many of the people. Even in such a case, however, when the people speak of the image as the god, in their minds they appear to have the same idea that more advanced people have when they think of the bodily form of a friend as being the person, and yet after his death would not consider the lifeless body to be the one whom they had known.

The popular idea that these Dravidians are worshipers of "stocks and stones" needs, therefore, considerable modification. It is true that, while the spirit is supposed to be residing in the image, the image itself receives the worship. At such a time one who is rash enough to take liberties with such an image will certainly think that the image itself is the god, for the worshipers would defend it or resent any familiarities most fanatically.

THE MEANING OF THE SACRIFICES. The fundamental idea of the sacrifices is undoubtedly that of propitiation. The spirits are

[41] *The Manual of Administration of the Madras Presidency*, p. 81, says that images are not essential to demon-worship, and have been adopted from Brahmanism.

bloodthirsty, and so blood is shed before them. The more terrible ones must have rivers of blood running before them.[42] Often the *pujari* drinks some of the blood. The reason for this is that the *pujari* for the time represents the goddess, and through him her desire for blood is satisfied.[43] In the case of some of the Saktis, blood is poured into their mouths. Bloody rice is scattered about the fields by farmers hoping that the devils will thus be satisfied and not molest the crop. It is very evident that it is blood which the spirits want.

Bishop Whitehead[44] thinks that the explanation commonly given, that the god takes the essence while the worshiper eats the body, is not satisfactory. He suggests that this idea may be a very recent addition from the Roman Catholic doctrine of transsubstantiation. Neither explanation seems really necessary, so far as the sacrifices of animals are concerned. It is blood which the spirit wants and blood which is offered to it. It is quite probable that originally it was the life as symbolized by the blood which was desired. It is the giving of life to redeem life. The blood is the life in the thought of these people as well as in that of the Hebrews, and when the fowl or animal is beheaded and the blood is poured out, the desire for life is satisfied.

When we go further and ask why life is desired by the spirit,

[42] In one place in the Nalamalli Hills the blood is poured into a stone trough in front of the image. When a dog comes and drinks it they think the goddess has entered the dog and is satisfied. This is one of the more terrible devils and is worshiped by the thieves. There is probably some connection between such worship and that of Kali by the Thugs. See *The Confessions of a Thug,* by Colonel Meadows Taylor, London, 1906, p. 27.

[43] In such worship as that of Ankamma described on page 24, I have tried to connect the dressing as a woman and riding in the midst of impaled animals with such a ceremony as carrying the vitals in the mouth for the purpose of frightening away other spirits. I have not been able to establish the point, however. The entire testimony is to the effect that the *pujari* dressed as a woman represents the goddess, that he is for the time the incarnation of the goddess, and so she is getting the benefit of the blood which he drinks, and the impaled animals are sacrifices to her.

[44] *Madras Government Museum, Bulletin,* V, no. 3, p. 179.

we are in the region of speculation. It seems quite probable that the reason is the same as that which leads to human sacrifices, or to the burying of wife, weapons, etc., with a dead man. The spirits of these things will be needed in the future world. So with the Dravidian sacrifices, the god is the spirit of some one who has lived on earth, and the spirit of the sacrifice is needed to be of some service in the spirit realm, as the body would be of service on earth.

There is, however, another feature of the worship which does not yield to such an explanation, and that is the sacrificial meal. In the case of the milder goddesses this is a very constant feature. This sacrificial meal is usually a time of merrymaking and good fellowship. As already pointed out in the discussion of totemism,[45] this feast probably originated in the idea common among all primitive people, that eating together cements friendship. It is peace and friendship with the goddess which are desired.

In some way, it is thought, the goddess also is partaking. In some of the sterner forms of worship the *pujari* eats in the name of the goddess, and as in every case it is the attendants of the goddess who have the right to eat what is offered to her, it may be considered that they too eat in her name. I do not see, however, sufficient reason for rejecting the explanation commonly given by the people, that the goddess takes the spiritual part of the food or its essence or spiritual strength. One of the chief features of the ceremonies for the dead is the placing of food on the grave of the departed for his spirit. The spirit world is very real to the Dravidian, and as he believes the air to be full of spirits with all kinds of powers, he would see no difficulty in the food also having a spiritual essence which these spirits utilize.

Origin of Dravidian Gods. The Puranic legends which have been related in connection with the Dravidian gods make them out to be incarnations of the Hindu Saktis.[46] The Hindu Sakti

[45] See page 129.

[46] Ziegenbalg, *Genealogy of South Indian Gods*, Madras, 1869, pp. 146, 147, says that the story told him by a Brahman was that the local goddesses existed at first in the abode of the gods, and originated from Parasakti, another name for Durga. They became proud and arrogant, and so were

is the personification of the energy of the Hindu god in the person of his wife. The Dravidian Sakti, however, is any female ghost which has evil powers. Moreover the Sakti worship of the *Tantras* has almost nothing in common with that of the Dravidians.[47] No original connection between the two has yet been established. The Brahmanic influence which has attempted to fuse the two cults has identified Dravidian spirit worship with Hindu Sakti worship. The stories which have been given all show Brahmanic origin and the wish to connect the two lines of legends. No local story about any one of these gods shows any relation to the Puranic stories.

The fact that the Dravidian deities are so generally female[48]

banished to the earth where they were given the office of protecting men from demons, among whom they reign as queens. If they do this work faithfully, at the end of the *Kali yugamu* they will again be reinstated in their former position. Ziegenbalg appears here to be speaking only of the Seven Sisters.

[47] See page 39.

[48] There is occasionally a male god among the Dravidians as Potu Razu (see page 24) and Aiyanar. This latter is an important demon in the Tamil country. He has authority over the other demons and is provided with pottery horses to ride on his night raids. He is said to be the Venkatasu of the Telugus. The story of his birth is Puranic. It is that there was once a terrible demon named Bhasmasura. Siva promised him that everything he touched should be turned to ashes. The demon now tried to touch Siva himself, but he fled. Vishnu now took the form of a fascinating young woman, and the demon wanted her. The young woman ordered him to bathe and put oil on his head. He did so and was turned to ashes. Siva now asked Vishnu to become that young woman again for his benefit. Vishnu consented, and Aiyanar is their child. See *Gazetteer of South Arcot,* I, p. 99; Oppert, *Original Inhabitants of India,* p. 505. The demon, Kattan, is another male god of importance. See Ziegenbalg, *Genealogy of South Indian Gods,* pp. 160–163, and Oppert, *The Original Inhabitants of India,* p. 483. He is said to be the son of an adulterous Brahman woman and was brought up by a pariah. He violated all the women in his region. The men could not catch him, so he impaled himself on a stake, and becoming a terrible devil was made a servant of Mariayamma.

Such male gods as these are so very exceptional as to be noteworthy. In the case of Potu Razu and Kattan they are not independent, but are servants of the female gods. These few exceptions emphasize the preponderance of female deities.

would seem to connect them with the Hindu Saktis. It is quite probable that the same causes have developed female deities in both cults. The reason for the Dravidian deities being female is probably nothing very profound, and is not especially complimentary to the female sex among the Dravidians. The qualities which bring these goddesses the worship of the people are their most undesirable ones. These qualities are quarrelsomeness, vindictiveness, jealousy, and similar attributes.

It is a generally admitted fact in South India that it is the Dravidian women rather than the men who are adepts in the use of bad language and vigorous terms of defamation. Aryan and Mohammedan influence has somewhat suppressed the Dravidian women, yet it is commonly known that these women usually secure their own way, and that by methods not always pleasant. Their curses, too, are not unknown, and are much feared. When such a woman attains the freedom and power of a spirit, and there is reason to believe that she has returned to the scenes of her life, it is considered wise to propitiate her. The entire explanation is in all probability simply that the feminine characteristics of the Dravidians are such as to make their ghosts more feared than those of the men.[49]

The fundamental conception of the Dravidians with regard to the origin of their gods is without doubt that they are the spirits of departed people. The basis is the primitive belief in ghosts. The Dravidians have a great fear of ghosts of all kinds, regardless of what their earthly career has been.[50]

[49] The worship of the female Dravidian deities is very commonly spoken of as mother worship. This is the term used by Monier-Williams (*Brahmanism and Hinduism*, pp. 222–229). He admits that many of their functions are anything but maternal. Hopkins (*The Religions of India*, p. 415) uses the same term and then proceeds to describe local demons. At times the people will call a beneficient deity a *tali* or mother, but this is unusual. The *perantalu* often seem to be considered as benevolent to some extent. The general idea, however, which the Dravidians have of their gods is not at all maternal, and I believe that mother worship did not originate with them either as to the name or the conception. It comes from the Hindu idea of the Saktis who are the wives of the gods, and so may properly be considered to be mothers.

[50] *Census of Madras*, 1891, III, p. 60, remarks that there is very little

There are many customs practised by the people to prevent the return of a ghost after the burial ceremony. The Lambadi people allow only one person from each family to go to a funeral. After performing the last rites those who have followed the corpse steal quietly back to the camp by various paths. Immediately they break camp and move far away so that the ghost of the departed one may not follow them. Some other classes make a hole in the wall or roof of the house through which the dead body is taken. This opening is then closed up so that the ghost may not be able to return. The Valaiyans place a pot of dung and water, also a broom and firebrand, at various places along the road to the burying ground to prevent the return of the ghost.[51]

In the funeral ceremonies and other rites for the dead such as the *taddinum,* there are many acts performed with the one intention of preventing the ghost from returning. On the last day of the ceremonies the friends go to a sacred *jammi* tree and taking little pots in their hands, they pretend to throw something into the air. This is probably a remnant of a former food-offering to the spirit of the departed. This done, they put out the lights, and in perfect quietness come again to the house by various paths so that the spirit may not follow them. After they have arrived at the house some outsider often appears and apparently becoming possessed with a spirit asserts that it is the spirit of the dead person which has come upon him. A substantial present persuades the possessed person to leave. Otherwise the spirit would probably ask for worship. This final act seems to assure the people that they are forever rid of the ghost of the dead person.

Among the Gulgulias there is a custom of pouring liquor into the mouth of the corpse. A chicken is killed and is then burned and the ashes thrown into an irrigation tank, in the hope that the ghost will be satisfied.[52] The Palyans, a jungle tribe, leave the

nature worship among the Dravidians. "Nature worship is Aryan. Among the Dravidians, on the other hand, religion seems to have commenced with a belief in ghosts."

[51] *Gazetteer of Tanjore District,* I, p. 77.

[52] *Census of 1901,* p. 407.

body unburied, and avoid the place for months through fear of the ghost.[53]

In other cases the footprints of the mourners are swept away so that the ghost may not be able to track them. The people shake out their clothes fearing that a ghost may be in hiding. At times a stone is set up to impede the progress of the ghost.[54] The soul is considered to be dependent upon the living, and so is provided for, or it will return and do harm.[55]

The ghosts which become deities are generally those of personages about whose death there has been something peculiar. Wicked people, especially if they have died because of their sins, have an open sesame to the pantheon. It is because their ghosts are dangerous and so are feared.[56]

Another class of ghosts which is feared, and whose members easily become deities are those who have died violent deaths,

[53] *Gazetteer of Madura District,* p. 105.

[54] This suggests the origin of an idol. It may be thought that the ghost will remain by the stone, or perhaps that as offerings are placed by the stone the ghost will come no further. The step from this to considering the stone to be the representation of the spirit would be a short one. The custom of placing rags in a tree may be connected with this. The *Gazetteer of South Arcot,* I, p. 102, says that no one seems to know the reason for the custom, but the people think it will do some good. Travelers, especially, tear a piece from their clothes and leave it in the tree. This may be so that no spirit may follow them. The spirit will stop to examine the rag in the tree and so lose the scent. In Madras within a short distance of the Government Museum is a furlong stone which has *botlu* placed on it. Perhaps this too is to stay the progress of some pursuing spirit.

[55] *Census of India,* 1901, p. 407.

[56] In the Nizam's Dominions there lived recently a much feared rajah. Since his death he is worshiped as a malignant demon who gives cholera, etc. Associated with him is a female ghost, Ramamma, who was his concubine. *Manual of Kurnool District,* p. 153. A curious custom is reported in the *Manual of Administration of the Madras Presidency,* I, p. 81. to the effect that because it is thought that spirits of criminals executed for their crimes will return, the hamstrings of the criminals are severed to prevent their traveling. The *State Manual of Travencore,* II, p. 55, says that many of the demons originate from those whose lives have been cut short by an untimely death. The spirit fills out its existence as a demon. The only difficulty with this theory is that as a demon the spirit never seems to finish its existence, but is immortal.

women who have died in childbirth, and any persons who have received marked injustice while on earth. It is thought that these people will have a grudge against the world which used them so badly, and so will return to get satisfaction.[57]

The ghosts of the Perantalus[58] apparently are not feared at first, but are worshiped because they did good while on earth. They become the milder and more beneficent of the goddesses, yet because of the general tendencies of Dravidian worship, the more bloody ceremonies are often present, and in time many of them come to be feared but little less than are the other demons.[59]

Morality of the Dravidian Religion. To one who for the first time comes into contact with the Dravidian religious ceremonies, they seem shocking and terrible. Comparing them with the ceremonies of Hinduism he is inclined to feel that the Dravidian rites represent the very acme of immoral "heathenism,"

57 I place here the deification of women dying in childbirth, for it seems the best explanation. What is more unjust than that a woman should lose her life in giving life to another? From the human point of view there is no explanation, and such a woman, it is thought by the Dravidians, will not be in a good mood toward the living.

58 In the Vizagapatam District Perantalu worship is very common. They are usually worshiped as *gramma devatalu*, or village goddesses, but have no influence over epidemics. In this district little is known of the local histories of the goddesses, which appears to indicate that they have come from further south. See *Gazetteer of Vizagapatam District*, I, p. 315.

59 *The Manual of Administration of the Madras Presidency*, p. 71, says that ancestor worship among the Dravidians began with fear of the shades of the ancestors. This is no doubt true wherever ancestor worship is found. As has been seen in the preceding pages, the deity is very seldom an ancestor. Ancestor worship is more Brahmanic than Dravidian. Sir Alfred Lyall (*Asiatic Studies*, First Series, p. 49) argues that the gods of the aboriginal tribes originate in the worship of living people. He says that the human personality impresses them so powerfully that they worship people while living, and the spirits of the same people after they have died. The foregoing investigations cast considerable doubt on this explanation. No instances have been found of a person being worshiped while living and also after death. It is the Brahmanic religion which teaches the worship of living people, that is, the worship of Brahmans. Among the Dravidians the absence of the worship of people and of human personality appears to be a marked feature.

while those of Brahmanic Hinduism have something of refinement and charm. A closer study shows, however, that while the Dravidian ceremonies are more shocking, their system does not contain so many immoralities as does that of the Brahmans.[60]

In Brahmanical Hinduism we find many most debasing customs which are condemned by no one more strongly than by the leading Hindu reformers themselves. The debauchery of many of their festivals, the shamelessness of many places of pilgrimage, the attachment of dancing girls to the temples with all which that implies, the lives of many of the religious mendicants, the unmentionable things in connection of the worship of the *lingam*, the proceedings in temples which women visit to pray for offspring: all these things are not denied by Hindus.

None of these immoralities has any counterpart in Dravidian worship. The night orgies may be hideous, but the very nature of the devil worship at night prevents other vice. The coming together of great crowds of people at festival times quite likely leads to more or less sin, but these festivals are pure compared with many of the festivals of Hinduism. The Dravidian *pujaris* have not the power over the people which the Brahman priests

[60] *Madras Government Museum, Bulletin*, V, no. 3, pp. 176, 177. "The Brahmanical system has sunk to lower depths than have been reached by the cruder religion of the village people. The worship of the village deities contains much that is physically repulsive. The details of the buffalo sacrifice are horrid to read about, and still worse to witness, and the sight of a *pujari* parading the streets with the entrails of a lamb round his neck and its liver in his mouth would be to us disgusting; and doubtless there is much drunkenness and immorality connected with the village festivals; while the whole system of religion is prompted by fear and superstition, and seems almost entirely lacking in anything like a sense of sin or feelings of gratitude toward a higher spiritual Power. But still it is also true, setting aside a few local customs in the worship of the village deities, there is nothing in the system itself which is so morally degrading and repulsive as the *lingam* worship of the Sivaites, or the marriage of girls to the god, and their consequent dedication to a life of prostitution among the Vaishnavites. If the worship of Siva and Vishnu has risen to greater heights, it has also sunk to lower moral depths than the less aesthetic worship of the *grama-devatas*."

possess, and so have less opportunity to turn their spiritual authority to carnal purposes.

The Dravidian system of religion may be said, indeed, to be non-moral rather than immoral.[61] Moral considerations do not enter into it at all. The propitiation of the village goddess is not to expiate moral lapses, but in so far as it has anything at all to do with conduct it is to make peace with her for any failure in her worship. In connection with their religion no one thinks of such a thing as reward for moral action or punishment for immoral conduct.

In the accounts of the formation of Dravidian deities it has been made evident that the immoral person is the one most likely to be deified. This fact may produce the impression that immorality is not condemned but rather sanctioned. It must be admitted that this making a god of the worst sinner may lead to approval of evil deeds, for the one who has sinned is the hero, and those who have brought just punishment upon him or her are the ones who have reason to fear. The influence of such ideas certainly is not good. In the deification of such evil doers, however, the moral question does not have any place. It is not because the man was a sinner that he became a god, but because

[61] *Census of India,* 1891, para. 99, p. 60: "There is very little connection between the religion and the morality of the people of the Madras Presidency. Their religion concerns itself with the ways to avoid or remove evil, but the idea that wicked conduct will be punished or good conduct obtain its reward in a future state is hardly to be found at all in the purely Dravidian religion. The fear of hell and the hope of heaven appear in the Puranic beliefs, but this doctrine has very little currency beyond the Brahmans and a few of the higher castes, and even among these the moral code of their religion is but vaguely known and of no great influence. Nearly every Hindu pays allegience to some *guru* or spiritual teacher, but the energies of their instructions are for the most part confined to teaching *mantrams* that are unintelligible to the pupil, and not always understood by the master, to performing ceremonial acts . . . and lastly to the collection of funds. The functions of the domestic priests are entirely ceremonial, and little if any religious instruction is given by the parents. The morality of the Hindus, indeed, is a matter of caste and not of religion, and misconduct is punished by the caste council, and not by the spiritual teacher."

such a man is thought to be more terrible and more unscrupulous than others, and so his ghost is feared the more.

In the matter of cheating and deceiving the gods we see simply a reflection of the everyday actions of the people among themselves. The Dravidian religion has no moral sanctions. It is simply a method of dealing with powerful spirits, the greater number of which are malignant. The religion reflects the morality of the people, and is in no way responsible for it.

# BIBLIOGRAPHY


## I. *Government and other Official Publications.*

Gazetteer of Anatapur District, 1905.
Gazetteer of Godavary District, 1907.
Gazetteer of Madura District, 1906.
Gazetteer of South Arcot, 1906.
Gazetteer of Trichinoply District, 1907.
Gazetteer of Vizagapatam District, 1907.
Imperial Gazetteer of India, 1886.
Journal of the Anthropological Society of Bombay, vols. I, II.
Kurnool District Manual, 1886.
Nellore District Manual, 1873.
Madras Government Museum; Bulletins IV, 3, 4; V, 3.
Manual of Administration of the Madras Presidency, 1885.
Reports on the Indian Census, 1891, 1901, 1911.
State Manual of Travencore, 1906.

## II. *General Works.*

Baden-Powell, B. H., *Village Communities in India,* London, 1908.
Barth, A., *The Religions of India,* London, 1882.
Bose, Shib Chundur, *The Hindus as They Are,* Calcutta, 1883.
Caldwell, R., *A Comparative Grammar of the Dravidian or South Indian Family of Languages,* London, 1875.
Clough, Emma Rauschenbusch, *While Sewing Sandals,* New York, 1899.
Crooke, William, *Things Indian,* New York, 1906.
*The Popular Religion and Folklore of Northern India,* Westminster, 1896.
*The Northwest Provinces of India,* London 1897.
Dubois, The Abbé J. A., *Hindu Manners, Customs and Ceremonies,* Oxford, 1899.
Fausbøll, V., *Indian Mythology according to the Mahabharata,* London, 1903.
Farquahar, J. A., *A Primer of Hinduism,* London, 1911.
Fergusson, James, *Tree and Serpent Worship,* London, 1868.
Jones, J. P., *India, Its Life and Thought,* New York, 1908.
Hopkins, Edward Washburn, *The Religions of India,* London, 1895.
Ketkar, Shridhar V., *Hinduism, Its Formation and Future,* London, 1911.
Lyall, Sir Alfred C., *Asiatic Studies,* First Series, London, 1907.
Mateer, Samuel, *Travencore and its People,* London, 1871.

Mitchell, J. Murray, *Hinduism, Past and Present*, London, 1897.
*The Great Religions of India*, London, 1905.
Monier-Williams, Sir Monier, *Brahmanism and Hinduism*, London, 1891.
Moor, E., *The Hindu Pantheon*, Madras, 1864.
Müller, F. Max, *Lectures on the Origin of Religion*, London, 1891.
*India, What it can teach Us*, London, 1892.
*Ancient Sanskrit Literature*, Edinburgh, 1860.
Murdock, J., *The Religious Sects of the Hindus*, Madras, 1904.
*Hindu and Mohammedan Festivals*, Madras, 1904.
Oman, J. Campbell, *Brahmans, Theists, and Muslims of India*, London, 1909. *Cults, Customs, and Superstitions of India*, London, 1908.
Oppert, Gustav, *The Original Inhabitants of India*, Westminster, 1893.
Padfield, J. E., *The Hindu at Home*, Madras, 1908.
Pandian, J. B., *Indian Village Folk*, London, 1898.
Paupa Rao Naidu, M., *The Criminal Tribes of India*, II, Madras, 1905.
Sherring, M. A., *The Sacred City of the Hindus*, London, 1868.
Smith, Vincent A., *Ancient India*, Madras, 1911.
Stacker, J. Fr., *The Arsenal*, Madras, 1910.
Taylor, Wm., *Oriental Manuscripts*, Madras, 1835.
Thurston, Edgar, *Omens and Superstitions of Southern India*, London, 1912.
*Castes and Tribes of Southern India*, Madras, 1908.
Ward, W., *View of the History, Religion and Literature of the Hindus*, London, 1818.
Wilkins, W. J., *Hindu Mythology*, Calcutta, 1882.
*Modern Hinduism*, Calcutta, 1900.
Ziegenbalg, B., *The Gods of Malabar*, Madras, 1869.

### III. *Sacred Books of the Hindus.*

*Atharva Veda*, translated by R. T. H. Griffith, Benares, 1895.
*Bhagavadgita*, translated by F. Max Müller, *Sacred Books of the East*, vol. viii, Oxford, 1908.
*Mahabharata*, translated by Pratapa Chandra Ray, Calcutta, 1893.
*Ramayana*, translated by R. T. H. Griffith, Benares, 1895.
*Rigveda*, translated by R. T. H. Griffith, Benares, 1896.
*Vishnu Purana*, translated by H. H. Wilson, London, 1865.

### IV. *Sanskrit and Telugu Works.*

*Agni Purana*, Madras, 1909.
*Bhagavata Purana*, Madras, 1892.
*Durga Sapta Shati*, in *Markandaya Purana*, Bangalore, 1893.
*Murali Mahathmam*, Jupoodi Sanjeevarow, Secunderabad, 1904.
*Padma Purana*, Madras, 1909.
*Sree Mad Bagavata*, Madras, 1893.

# INDEX